S0-AHD-707

Reason
in Pastoral Counseling

Reason in Pastoral Counseling

by
PAUL A. HAUCK

THE WESTMINSTER PRESS
Philadelphia

Book Design by
Dorothy Alden Smith

Published by The Westminster Press®
Philadelphia, Pennsylvania

PRINTED IN THE UNITED STATES OF AMERICA

Library of Congress Cataloging in Publication Data

Hauck, Paul A
Reason in pastoral counseling.

Bibliography: p.
1. Pastoral counseling. 2. Pastoral psychology.
I. Title.
BV4012.2.H37 253.5 72-76436
ISBN 0-664-20945-9

To those fair delights:

Marcie,
Kathy, Melanie, and Stephanie

Contents

Preface

THE NEW AGE THAT IS DAWNING CALLS ALL MEN OF THE cloth to see a new sunrise of their high purpose. The strong fibers that held together the fabric of Christianity have been strained by the weight of modern scholarship. Dogma is yielding to doubt, old attitudes to new, past purposes to greater visions. This revolution has placed today's pastor in the front ranks during some of the greatest changes in religion and society in centuries. The pastor has the rare opportunity to be part of this historic movement. His alternative is to be lost, a mere critic, blind to the call of his times.

Among the changes he is called upon to make are those which require a new attitude toward earthly life itself. He is called upon to recognize the essential worth of earthly life and the dignity of the person in whom that life resides. The focus on earthly happiness calls for a greater awareness of man's emotional life and of the means that give him an opportunity to realize that goal. The day is past when modern man, his shoulders burdened with the day's concerns, is content to seek out his minister and to accept homespun philosophy and a prayer session as a solution to his distress. To meet the demands now being put upon him, the pastor must acquaint himself with counseling as it is done by professionals. He must enter the arena himself. Most importantly, he must keep an open mind toward new techniques, especially when they appear to clash with his faith.

Reason, critically employed, has seldom been a friend of faith. This book has been written to demonstrate two trends: that reason is being employed in counseling as a new weapon against emotional pain, and that it need not disrupt faith.

I came upon this new psychotherapeutic system purely by chance. The leader of a clinical course to be given in the 1964 series of the Post-doctoral Institute for graduate psychologists, scheduled in the late summer at Temple University, Philadelphia, became ill. His course was scratched. Plans to attend the Institute having been formed, I made a hasty choice to become a member for four days in the course on rational-emotive psychotherapy, to be conducted by Dr. Albert Ellis. Chance is fickle; how often it leads one on to expect little and surprises him with a treasure!

It was only some months later, after having the opportunity to use reason in my private and public practice, that I began to realize what a lucky choice I had made in Philadelphia. Since then, my zeal for this system has (with a few reservations) intensified to the degree that I have wanted to share my experience of rebirth as a clinical psychologist with others. Toward that end I volunteered my services to Dr. Ellis and the Institute for Rational Living in New York City to set up a journal for intelligent laymen and professionals. The first issue of *Rational Living* appeared in the Spring of 1966 with Robert Wolf as my assistant editor. Having succeeded in launching the project, I resigned as editor and applied my free time to revising the manuscript of the book I had written for Libra Press, *The Rational Management of Children.*

After the manuscript was accepted for publication I wrote a series of lectures for seminars to ministerial groups. They were so well received that I was encouraged to expand and reorganize them in book form. The final product was REASON IN PASTORAL COUNSELING.

My greatest drive for writing this book, however, was the desire to show the clergy that its first impressions of the system are likely to be erroneous ones. Because of Dr. Ellis' antireligious opinions and unorthodox sexual views, to say nothing of his startlingly emotive language, it is difficult to see clearly what he is offering. As do most persons upon first being introduced to rational-emotive psychotherapy (also called rational-emotive therapy, or RET), I had a strong tendency to discount it as cultish and unprofessional. The thought that RET principles might even harmonize with Christian belief at many important points was indeed slow to be realized. It was only after sifting the man's style from his ideas that I came to see that Dr. Ellis had indeed suggested ways of making Christianity workable. This applies not to all of his views by any means, but to many. Those principles which I feel are usable for Christianity are dealt with in the following pages.

Several acknowledgments are in order here. For their generous help in typing much of this material when it was first conceived as a series of lectures, I am grateful to Mrs. Henrietta Van Hyfte, Mrs. Alice Wing, Mrs. June Nickus, and Miss Lena Cooley. To Mrs. Polly Mann, Pastor William O'Neill, and Pastor Fred LeShane, I am especially thankful for their reading the rough draft of this book and offering many worthwhile suggestions. A special note of thanks goes to Sisters Annette Walters and Ritamary Bradley for help with the final draft. Rector of the seminary at St. Ambrose College, Father L. D. Soens, was most encouraging during a period of doubt, and he offered a number of helpful suggestions.

Mrs. Gladys Leach typed the final manuscript and, as is always her way, she was eager, efficient, and reliable.

I am most grateful to Dr. Ellis and his teachings in psychotherapy, which enabled me to have a new sense of self-confidence and self-discipline, so crucial in any writing endeavor.

My wife and family graciously accepted the time my writing took away from them. This was needed and greatly appreciated.

P.A.H.

Introduction

THE PRESENT EPOCH IS SEEING A NEW INTEREST IN PASTORAL counseling as a distinct discipline. Though he has always been sought after in times of emotional distress, and though he has always been a pastoral counselor by demand, the clergyman has usually considered this a function that was thrust upon him, for which he was poorly trained, and that was of secondary importance to such tasks as serving the Spirit, building a church, teaching theology, or administering the sacraments. Yet so persistent has been the demand for his advice on marital conflicts or interpersonal problems that the pastor has of necessity reappraised his role. During the past two decades, he has begun to acquaint himself with such fields as psychology and psychiatry in order to be better equipped.

The present stir in pastoral counseling is regrettably caused by only a minority of pastors. Behind the activity of the few who are acquiring a scientific knowledge of counseling stands a majority of pastors who, for several reasons, are only looking on. In reality, as my own experience has shown, a great number of ministers feel that counseling should be left to the professional psychotherapists; that secular counseling detracts from the more worthwhile goal of caring for the spirit; that "curing" neurotics is a medical concern; or that traditional religious approaches are quite sufficient and do not require new techniques. Mental distress is viewed by this latter group as the product of sinful behavior and is dealt with in the same way as all sinful behavior: through religious education and prayer.

This group of "agnostics" tends to give lip service to the new counseling movement while proceeding unruffled and unchanged along its well-trodden ways. These men read the new books but practice the old techniques. They sit in seminars on counseling, but have no cases of their own to discuss. And others, unless the new approaches closely coincide with their theology, cannot sift what is meaningful and applicable from the new psychology for use in their own value systems. They turn their backs on all of it.

This state of affairs must and will change. The time for a realignment between religion and psychology is not far off, and the effort will be made. Those who sidestep this movement will find themselves lost in the unfamiliar theological climate of tomorrow.

It is my earnest belief that the relief of emotional distress as well as the control of destructive impulses is the rightful concern of everyone. The teacher has an obvious obligation to acquire a sound foundation in mental health. So does each parent. But what of the police, the courts, the politician? To create a truly Christian society it will be the duty of every person who reaches other souls to understand those souls and to know a great deal about helping them.

There are several special reasons why the clergyman has every right to enter actively into this struggle.

1. He, along with the family physician, is still in the majority of cases contacted first by persons in distress. Apparently it is more face-saving for a housewife to approach the minister about her marital difficulties (which she and he tacitly accept as being "normal" human problems) than it would be to admit that she and her husband are struggling neurotically with each other. The unspoken assumption she might have to make in seeking out a psychotherapist for her troubles is that she or her husband is "sick," "neurotic," or perhaps even "crazy." No such mental juggling is needed when counseling with a trusted friend or confidant of the family's. Thus, placed in a position that the professional therapist can only envy, the minister has the kind of ready-made atmosphere for counseling that other disciplines must often engineer.

Therefore, whether he wishes it or not, the pastor will continue for some time to be an important first link in a helping chain. If he assumes this challenge, he can play a vital part toward the relief of much unchristian behavior motivated by neurotic motives. If he fails to accept this challenge, he will eventually be ignored and his church will be the loser, to say nothing of the whole Christian cause.

2. The sheer weight of the enormous amount of neurotic behavior daily displayed by all sorts of people demands that everyone be called upon to help.[1] A community threatened with a flood or forest fire may have to press into service every available able-bodied person. Though less dramatic, the plague of destructive behavior in our society is omnipresent and simply cannot be dealt with effectively by a small, however well trained, group of professionals. Every one of us is mildly neurotic from time to time, including the psychotherapists. Serious dis-

ruption due to neurosis, however, affects between twenty and thirty percent of the population.[2] The problem is enormous. This fact alone makes its alleviation the just concern of us all. For a better world we simply cannot argue over prerogatives or niceties of professional privilege. While such disputes shackle capable hands, the problem grows worse. The techniques are available; they are teachable and consonant with most of the prevailing religious doctrines. The need is clearly evident, yet many ministers are reluctant to use these techniques.

3. If need does not sway the doubtful, let us look to example. Christ never confined his work solely to teaching. The relief of human suffering, whether spiritual or physical, was among his greatest concerns. Was it because he failed to differentiate physical from spiritual well-being? Was it because he realized a kinship between proper behavior and a spirit that was at peace with itself? I believe so. And I am further convinced that a moral and religious life is easier to lead when these goals are not dulled by pain, whatever the kind. Emotional pain is among the worst that can be experienced. It works against self-respect, love of one's neighbors, and other charitable acts. It creates impatience with others and intolerance for their fallibilities. It seeks to deal with them in a spiteful, painful manner.[3]

This is not the Way. The whole person must be our concern. He cannot be divided into compartments, each under the sole care of a specialist. Though we live in an age of increasing specialization because of the proliferation of knowledge, we must be aware of the real dangers in never dealing with man as a total being. The center of the whole lies always in his philosophical beliefs. And who is more concerned with them than the minister? Let the physician operate on the ulcer, the dentist fill the decaying molar, the English teacher correct the faulty grammar, and the accountant advise on the reckless spending habits. But where does this organism go? And why? How should it conduct itself while living out its brief stay on earth? After the ulcer, the molar, the sentence construction, and the finances are in order, we are still left with a human being who has no direction or purpose unless a larger scheme can fit all the diverse elements into a plan. Religion has always regarded itself as knowing what that plan was. Psychology and psychiatry are now recognizing the deep wisdom in much of our everyday religious teachings. But religion has falsely believed it also has the means by which it could teach man to follow the path laid down in the Scriptures.

The rising number of emotionally disturbed people, not only within the population at large but also among the ministers themselves, creates grave doubts that the churches have that complete answer. True, the professions do not have the total answer either. But at least they are closer to achieving some of the goals set forth in the gospel than are the ministers. Religion has prescribed a destination for man; psychology is discovering how it can be reached. Clergymen who refuse to familiarize themselves with the latter will seldom have the satisfaction of aiding others to the former. They are part and parcel of one process: the good life. On what grounds can the minister turn his back on any possibility, any suggestion, any school of thought that might help him in his mission? If he will make the whole person his concern, as Christ did, instead of dealing only with that person's soul, as he has done traditionally, the pastor will be much closer to achieving his noble mission.

4. Many ministers are honestly reluctant to engage in the counseling of emotional problems because of their belief that neurosis is a disease entity and, therefore, the rightful and exclusive concern of the physician. Indeed, the medical model of emotional distress has been widely held by psychology and sociology, to say nothing of the general public.

That this should be so is quite understandable. Medicine has responded to the call of the pained from the beginning of primitive social life. Throughout history it has been the physician who has made the dramatic contributions toward the alleviation of mental pain. The most noteworthy example in the recent past is the work of Sigmund Freud, who, though he regarded himself as a psychologist with respect to his work on analysis, was still very influential in propagating the idea that neurosis is a disease. And why should he not? Did his patients not have paralyzed arms or legs? Were they not anxious, did they not sleep poorly and have upset stomachs? And are these conditions not associated with the nerves?

As with all men, Freud was a product of his times and could not see beyond his era in all respects. His great contributions regarding unconscious life attest to his vision, a superior vision to be sure, but not infallible. His work on the ego has been expanded by grateful students to a point where today the cognitive (reasoning) processes are receiving the same attention once given the affective (emotional) processes. And with a resurgence of interest in the intellect as a source of controlling emotions, the shift was gradually made from the familiar notion of treatment to the newer idea of relearning. Related conceptions have undergone similar transformations. The counselor joins the doctor in removing ignorance and in teaching new habits that modify behavior, rather than in prescribing medicines that are supposed to bring on cures.

Let us examine these statements in greater detail, because their comprehension is absolutely vital if the pastor is to have a satisfying rationale for doing counseling.

Mental illness is a slippery term referring to at least two kinds of distress: (*a*) emotional disturbance without bodily pain, and (*b*) emotional disturbance with (causing or caused by) bodily pain.

In the first case we have all the varied and numerous emotional reactions so common to our daily lives. Many of us are angry, depressed, or worried rather frequently without at the same time having a headache, ulcers, or serious insomnia. It is only infrequently that these daily emotions, in addition to being mentally painful, are *also* physically painful.

Why, then, should we regard each and every mental upheaval as a disease to which a doctor must attend? Though it has not been widely appreciated, the fact is being increasingly understood that emotional disturbance is not a medical issue at all *unless* a painful bodily dysfunction results. In that event the medical doctor has a prerogative only over the medical problem, while he *or someone else* can deal with the emotional distress.

As an analogy we might look to the automobile. It may have a torn fender and a defective engine. Though both conditions resulted from the same accident, their repair is best achieved in the hands of two specialists: the body man and the engine mechanic. Granted, one man skilled in both fields could do the complete repair work, but we consider this incidental to the fact that two separate tasks are involved and require two distinct skills, which may or may not be possessed by the same man.

It is the same with neurotics, psychotics, psychopaths, and the marginally adjusted. That this has been accepted (at least tacitly) is proven by the fact that nonmedical people have for years been doing excellent counseling and continue to do so. They are teachers in every sense of the word, whether they have recognized this fact or not. Even the physician assumes the role of a teacher when practicing psychotherapy, with the exception of those few moments when he is prescribing drugs or being obviously medically occupied.

The newer view of emotional distress regards it not as a disease but as faulty learning.[4] In place of the concept of "cured" we must substitute "modified," "corrected," or "learned." Instead of thinking of himself as a doctor or therapist, the counselor will regard himself as an educator and teacher. This shift in thinking demands that equally iconoclastic efforts be made over several other of our most deeply ingrained expressions. A clinic is more properly a school, a therapy hour a lesson, the office a classroom, and the patient a student.

Cast in this light the minister can readily see his rightful place. One of his functions has always been that of a teacher. Probably the greatest share of his work involves *instruction*. Why, then, should he be exempt from performing a service for which he has as much skill as most nonclerical counselors?

In the following pages we will undertake to place at the minister's disposal the tools by which this role can be realized. But he will need tolerance and courage to apply these methods to his religious framework, and he will need great patience to learn them.

Reason
in Pastoral Counseling

1
The Principles of Rational-Emotive Psychotherapy

THE PROPER STARTING POINT FOR UNDERSTANDING RATIONAL-emotive psychotherapy is with the *ABC Theory of Emotions*. This theory postulates that people become disturbed when they believe senseless, alarming, and disturbing ideas. These ideas are internalized, silent, conscious or unconscious comments that the person is making to himself. It is these ideas or beliefs that cause the disturbance rather than the event or other person connected with the ideas. Changing the thoughts to rational, logical, sensible ones and then behaving differently on the strength of these new beliefs causes the disturbances to wither away.

An emotion is a physical reaction to a mental stimulus. If we have angry thoughts, we feel angry. If we have alarming thoughts, we feel tense. If we blame ourselves, the result is depression. In every case the thought, whether known to the subject or not, precedes the feeling. Ellis has labeled this process the ABC Theory of Emotions. A is any event outside of ourselves. B is our attitude, opinion, belief—in short, our thinking about A. And C is the emotional reaction we have as a response—not to A, the event, but to B, the opinion about it.

The ABC Theory of Emotions: Mrs. Martin

Mrs. Martin was typical of my clients who immediately questioned the implications of this theory. After I explained it to her during our first counseling session she remarked, "Then according to your thinking, it's never others who upset me, but always myself?"

"That's right, Mrs. Martin," I added, "as long as other people aren't actually hurting you physically."

"Well, what about when my husband goes into one of his wild scenes and swears and calls me the vilest names? You surely don't mean that he isn't upsetting me then, do you?"

"Yes, I do. If he isn't giving you a black eye while he's screaming and bellowing at you, I insist he isn't upsetting you in the least."

"But, doctor," she protested, "you must be joking. Everyone knows that words can hurt. Why, it's only natural to get upset in such a situation."

"I agree it's natural all right. So is eating raw meat. That has nothing to do with it. The point you fail to see is that he has done nothing to you except throw a lot of ugly words at you, which you take seriously and use to stir up your own emotions. It is not your husband's arguing that can do you harm. It's at point B, your *thinking* about his arguing that causes your depression and anger at C. If you changed those alarming thoughts at B, you'd soon feel better. For example, what sort of nonsense do you tell yourself when he attacks you verbally?"

"I frankly don't tell myself anything. I only know I get mad and am very unhappy."

"Yes, but you must have had some mad and unhappy

thoughts to make you feel that way. The thought always comes before the feeling, whether you're aware of it or not. Try right now to imagine what you generally are thinking about when he starts a fight with you."

She thought a moment and said, "Let's see, I'm probably telling myself that I hate him for being so unfair and unreasonable and that's he's an awful, terrible person to treat me so badly."

"Anything else?" I urged.

"Then I probably think about how miserable I've been lately and how much I want him to love and approve of me but he won't. That really brings on the tears," she said with a sad smile.

"It seems to me, Mrs. Martin, that you've just proven my point. Can't you see how impossible it would be for you to feel any other way but angry and depressed after feeding yourself those disturbing thoughts? No one, I repeat, no one could conceivably remain calm during a scene with a husband as long as she kept telling herself such poison."

"And if I changed my thought, I'd change my feelings? I'd love my husband while he was calling me dirty names?"

"Almost. You wouldn't, of course, like what he said, but you could certainly like *him* nevertheless. Suppose you had told yourself sensible, logical thoughts such as: 'Poor fellow, there he goes again, making himself angry and spoiling another evening for himself. Well, that's too bad, but all his screaming won't hurt me unless I let it, so I might just as well stay calm until he gets over this. After all, it's his problem, not mine.' Now, if you had told yourself this kind of thing, can't you see how utterly impossible it would be to get disturbed next time?"

"I confess it sounds very reasonable, but almost too easy. All I'm supposed to learn is how to think calm thoughts and I'll never be upset again as long as I live?"

"It's not quite that easy, Mrs. Martin. You'll have to concentrate hard not to repeat your past thinking habits, and you'll slip many times along the way. However, if you do begin to question, seriously question, the neurotic junk you've been believing all along, you will most certainly begin to improve."

"It sounds almost too mechanical and too simple. I've tried to talk myself out of lots of upsetting feelings in the past and it hasn't worked."

"Technically, it isn't just what you think that upsets you. The thoughts that upset you are those thoughts which you *believe* to be true. That's the big difference. If you believe your husband is a demon because he speaks unkindly to you, you'll have to get upset if he continues after you ask him to stop. If, however, you have the thought that he is a demon but don't honestly believe it, then you won't be upset."

"So it isn't just what I tell myself that upsets me but what I believe, is that it?"

"True. The reason I go back to asking you to tell me what you are telling yourself is that all your beliefs are expressed in verbal symbols, or in silent words. That's what your thoughts are, aren't they?"

"I suppose so. If I want to think of something, I can't do it unless I use language, that is, words and sentences. These are the tools of my thinking, or talking to myself. And some of this thinking I believe and some I reject. Right?"

"Right, Mrs. Martin. The sensible and logical ideas you

have and accept will not upset you. The illogical, alarming, upsetting things you tell yourself may or may not upset you—depending on whether or not you believe them."

"I see it now," she blurted out. "In the past when I have tried to talk myself out of a disturbance and it didn't work, it wasn't because I was telling myself sensible things, but because I didn't believe what I was thinking. Is that right?"

"Precisely. You are probably talking to yourself on two levels. The one was conscious and healthy, while the other was unconscious and disturbing. For example, after getting into a fight with your husband, you may have told yourself consciously that he's not all bad, that the poor fellow can't help getting upset each week, and that none of his outbursts can really do you any great harm anyway. If you could have accepted these thoughts as being eminently and practically sound, you would have believed them and calmed down.

"In the past, however, you have subconsciously added other thoughts, which were sabotaging the good thinking you were doing on the surface. In addition to the thoughts that your husband is not all bad, you probably whispered the idea to yourself, 'Perhaps so, but he has more than his fair share of faults.' If you had the thought that he can't help being disturbed, because of the way he was raised, you probably countered it at a suppressed level with: 'I don't care how badly his folks raised him. I'm not his parents and why should I have to take the brunt of *their* mistakes.'

"You see, Mrs. Martin, what I'm trying to say is that mere talking to oneself is not enough reason to get upset or to calm down. It is only when we believe that our internalized irrational thoughts make sense, that they make us upset. It is only when we believe the rational things we are saying to ourselves, that we calm down."

"Then I apparently must try to reexamine the things I am telling myself about my husband and his arguing, and then refuse to let myself believe they all make sense. And that should get me over my anger and tension?"

"After you tell yourself sane thoughts which you then completely believe are sane, your emotional disturbance will be over," was my unequivocal answer.

This line of instruction went on for several weekly sessions, each time rephrased, and each time answering her questions and countering her objections. In our fifth hour she came in beaming a broad smile. "Doctor, something happened this week that I wouldn't have believed if it hadn't happened to me."

"What's that?"

"Just this past week my husband began getting irritable in his usual way and I knew he was just itching for a fight. He started arguing, finding fault and calling me the usual nasty names. Naturally I started to get angry and could feel myself getting hot under the collar, when I suddenly recalled what you've been telling me: 'His words can't hurt you, and if he dislikes you right now, so what? You can't expect him to be charming and delightful all the time. So calm down, Mrs. Martin. Straighten yourself out at B and your husband out there at point A won't be able to upset you in the slightest at point C.' "

"And it really worked, didn't it?" I asked.

"It certainly did. I sat there calm as a cucumber while he got madder and madder. It was a wonderful experience. The amazing thing about it was that I didn't merely keep quiet with a tight lid on my anger, as I've done so many times before. I actually had no anger at all that needed to be bottled up."

From that time on, Mrs. Martin was a changed woman, although her husband, whom I never saw, continued on his neurotic way. She learned to accept him as he was and to avoid hurting herself by letting him upset her.

If our disturbed feelings are created by our own thinking, what about our pleasant, happy emotions? Do we create them also? Yes, in the same way, by telling ourselves that something is lovely, beautiful, or funny. A joke, a comedy, a present, cannot please us unless we choose to let it please us. A bouquet of flowers is only a bouquet of flowers. If a man's wife is given them on her birthday, she will allow herself to be thrilled and happy. If her husband is offering flowers to soothe her for his adultery, they will probably be considered a cheap, despicable bribe. Again we see that *how* a person reacts to events is not determined by A, the flowers, but by B, the opinion about the flowers.

Eleven Irrational Ideas

As we have seen, the seat of neurotic disturbance rests with one's internalized thought processes, the B of the ABC theory. Obviously not every thought we have alarms or upsets us, only some. Do our upsetting thoughts fall into meaningful categories? Albert Ellis[5] has brilliantly delineated the common irrational ideas that cause us to suffer. They seem to be so obvious that one is inclined to say, "What's so new about that?" Actually, they are not obvious at all. These ideas are rigidly believed by millions of people throughout the world. Many times the RET counselor must spend most of his effort convincing a client that some of his pet notions and beliefs are actually ridiculous. Ellis' greatest contribution lies in the discovery that these beliefs *should* be questioned.

Thus far, he has concluded that all irrational ideas that cause mental pain fall under one of the following eleven, as outlined in his book *Reason and Emotion in Psychotherapy*.

IRRATIONAL IDEA NO. 1: *"The idea that it is a dire necessity for an adult human being to be loved or approved by virtually every significant other person in his community."* (The word "adult" should be particularly noted.)

People are constantly judging themselves by how others feel toward them. If they are liked, they conclude that they are worthwhile, valuable persons. If they are disliked, they accept this judgment as valid and dislike themselves. Believing falsely that our value of ourselves comes from others, they are naturally eager and sometimes driven to please these others in the expectation that they will thereby become "better" persons.

This is a foolish notion, for the simple reason that another person's evaluation of us is always determined by his own personality quirks. He is seldom the authority about us that we ourselves are. Probably he too is suffering under this irrational idea and may therefore feel he is worthless unless he has our approval or the approval of someone whom he greatly respects.

This idea is senseless also for another reason. It is the A in the ABC theory, and as such has no power to upset anyone unless he or she lets it be upsetting. Not being loved or liked is not a dire predicament, except perhaps in the case of children dependent on at least some approval from their parents. A wife who becomes depressed because her husband no longer loves her believes quite literally that she *needs* his love, when the truth is that his love is only very *desirable*. Life is always nicer when people we love return that love. But if they do not, we need not be mightily disturbed, since being unloved is hardly fatal. We have only to ask ourselves: "What if my spouse died tomorrow? He or she couldn't then give me any love or approval. Would that be the end of me?" Certainly not. Every day, spouses are lost by people who probably thought they needed more love than they received. None received all they wanted and most survived nicely. This could not happen if approval and love were a need. Any dire consequences resulting from unfulfilled wishes for approval are the result of a person's belief in Irrational Idea No. 1. When such people are shown in counseling how that idea is the cause of their misery, they often relinquish it and learn to think of the frustration calmly as just one of many unsatisfied wishes they have had throughout their lives.

IRRATIONAL IDEA NO. 2: *"The idea that one should be thoroughly competent, adequate, and achieving in all possible respects if one is to consider oneself worthwhile."*

This is without doubt one of the most strongly indoctrinated ideas our society supports. It assumes that one's value should be judged by one's achievements. The greater the achievement, the more worthwhile and superior the person feels himself to be. Likewise, failure is regarded as proof of one's inferiority. In the case of Irrational Idea No. 1, people evaluate themselves by the reactions of others, while with Irrational Idea No. 2 the evaluation of the person is of his own skills and is done by himself.

Our achievements do not reflect upon our worthiness, only upon our talents and experiences. The man who runs the mile under four minutes is not a better person than we. He is only a better runner. We need not feel inferior to him because we see ourselves as inferior athletes. To judge ourselves by our behavior puts an intolerable burden upon us to be perfect. This is the natural outcome of believing this idea. One is either perfect or one is bad, wicked, and evil.

This evaluation applies to neurotic and criminal behavior as well as to one's skills. The kleptomaniac is just as fine a person as you or I. As a human being he is bound to have some faults and one such fault might be stealing. It is senseless to claim that people *should not* misbehave and that they are bad because of this misconduct. Being born less than perfect means precisely that: *all* behavior will be imperfect at some time. People are going to rob, kill, and beat children. If they did not do this, they would by definition be infallible, and that is regrettably impossible. We do not say, for example, that people should not die. Why? Simply because to die is part of the meaning of being human. Only superhuman beings never die. As humans and mortals we *should* someday die. Likewise, not being gods, we act like people.

The suffering that this idea of achieved worth has caused is impossible to estimate. Practically everyone hates himself somewhat for his inadequacies. It will probably be some time before people learn to react to their errant ways with calmness and then devise ways to correct that behavior to avoid its repetition. Our common error is to focus, not on the mistake or its inception and correction, but on what terrible persons we are for having erred. We tend first to become depressed and later concerned about correcting the error. What a regrettable waste. Why not simply avoid this emotional detour and get right to correcting the problem if possible? By overthrowing Irrational Idea No. 2 this can be done.

IRRATIONAL IDEA NO. 3: *"The idea that certain people are bad, wicked, or villainous and that they should be severely blamed and punished for their villainy."*

Blame is here defined as a criticism of, and anger over a person's unacceptable behavior *and* the person as well. Since people are by nature imperfect, we must expect the worst from them. This is largely beyond their control. Only a continuous struggle with trial and error teaches us some modicum of saintly behavior. Therefore, it is totally logical to think of behavior as bad and wicked, and the person committing it as good, since he commits wrong deeds for at least one of three very good reasons. (1) He may be *stupid* or *mentally retarded* and hence may not know right from wrong. If Tom, a twenty-year-old mental defective, carelessly drops his cigarette in a farmer's barn causing it to burn to the ground, we can hardly consider him a villain despite his tragic and costly act. *He* is not bad, although his *behavior* was. (2) *Ignorance* is the second reason why people frequently commit wrong deeds. Had they better skills, greater ability, or more thorough training, they would surely not act in the erroneous fashion they do. The adolescent who shoots his hunting companion by mistake is also not an evil person, although his act is fatal. Perhaps he did not have knowledge of the safety catch, or how to carry his weapon. Can he be blamed for something he does not know? (3) The third reason people behave badly is their *neurotic personalities.* They have been taught by an irrational society to think and behave in self-defeating and inefficient ways. The amnesiac who deserts his family, wandering off to another life, has never been taught full responsibility and the technique whereby he can carry his burdens with equanimity. The murderer is also not wicked, although his act is. He too lacks the training required to handle problems by better means. He is not evil but disturbed, neurotic, infantile, etc. This, of course, does not relieve him of the responsibility for his acts. He committed the acts and must suffer the consequences. But it makes no sense to blame him for his shortcoming. In the majority of cases this only serves to make him hate himself and then feel *unable* to behave better.

The pastor will immediately be reminded of a number of Scriptural passages harmonious with this view. "Blessed are the merciful, for they shall obtain mercy" (Matt. 5:7). "Love your enemies" (Matt. 5:43-44). "Judge not, that ye be not judged" (Matt. 7:1). Such counsel is repeatedly found in the Gospels, arguing against Irrational Idea No. 3.

IRRATIONAL IDEA NO. 4: *"The idea that it is awful and catastrophic when things are not the way one would very much like them to be."*

People find it difficult to accept reality. Though it is perfectly reasonable to dislike reality, it is totally unreasonable to believe, therefore, that life must be different. Again, it is our perception of events, not events themselves, which makes them emotionally distressing. There is no reason why things must be our way, even though we are right. The party committing a supposed injustice against us probably believes as strongly in his rightness as we do in his wrongness.

Rather than create disturbances within ourselves over the events of the world, we should try to change, prevent, or modify these events. Only by being reasonably calm over a regrettable event is the person truly in a position to combat it effectively. The nervous and disturbed person often creates greater problems for himself because he deadens his problem-solving intelligence with worry and anxiety. Those events which cannot now, or ever, be changed, should be accepted philosophically instead of resentfully.

IRRATIONAL IDEA NO. 5: *"The idea that human unhappiness is externally caused and that people have little or no ability to control their sorrows and disturbances."*

This idea is irrational because it ignores the vital distinction between a frustration and a disturbance. The fact that one practically always follows the other does not vouch for its validity. A frustration is a disappointment—not having one's wishes or needs fulfilled. This is a daily, lifelong occurrence. How one reacts to the frustration, however, is a matter of personal choice by the subject. If he has been raised in a mature, adult fashion, he accepts frustrations as inevitable and does what he can to remove them or live with them. If he has been raised to have most of his desires fulfilled, he will become upset. Actually, though he does not realize it, he believes the frustration is *making* him upset, and that he has had no choice whatever in the matter. Yet one man will storm and fume over being discharged from work, while another will calmly look for new employment. A mother will be mightily upset at her child's messiness one day and ignore the same state of affairs the next. If the messiness really had the power to disturb her, it would do so on both days.

IRRATIONAL IDEA No. 6: "*The idea that if something is or may be dangerous or fearsome one should be terribly concerned about it and should keep dwelling on the possibility of its occurring.*"

To many, worry is thought to be essential to the eventual solution of their problems. They believe that they must feel anxiety over their problems if they are to attack them seriously. This is absolutely unnecessary, although people do manage their affairs while worrying. On closer inspection it will be seen that they manage whatever they do in spite of their worrying.

Problem-solving at the level of anxiety is an intellectual chore, whether it be taking a math test or singing before a group. A clear mind, closely focused on the issue obtains best results. The person who is telling himself, "Lord, what will happen if I don't make the grade?" or "Goodness, she isn't home yet? This is awful," is not really concentrating on the problem and its solution at all, but on the possibilities of all that may happen and how he will feel *if* they happen. All of us have seen individuals worry themselves sick and yet accomplish nothing toward the solution of their difficulties. It is what we *do* about things, not how much we worry over them, that makes a difference.

The worrier, burdening himself with needless anxiety and fear, actually often compounds his problems. If the worrying over a coming event is carried to extremes, an individual can incapacitate himself sufficiently to bring about the dreaded event. An adolescent having had one automobile accident can precipitate another by making herself nervous and disturbed as she drives with such thoughts as: "Wouldn't it be terrible if I had another accident? I must be careful, especially careful. I'd better not relax. I just can't repeat that mistake, I can't." One could almost be sure she *will* have another accident.

IRRATIONAL IDEA NO. 7: *"The idea that it is easier to avoid than to face certain life difficulties and self-responsibilities."*

As obvious as this may sound, it is astounding how many people do not really accept this thought as being irrational. To be sure, it is readily accepted intellectually as foolish, but in practice it is a problem to us all.

The difficulty lies in our being unable to deny ourselves immediate gratification for greater rewards later. The instant pleasure we obtain is so rewarding that it becomes difficult indeed to believe that we have thereby taken the more harmful course of action. Yet, it *is* true that avoiding our responsibilities and dodging difficult or unpleasant situations is *not* more beneficial to us. It is like a drug that deceptively lulls us into a quick sense of inner peace just before shattering our calm. The cost, however, is tremendous. People who avoid facing their problems to buy a moment's relief, pay enormously in later frustration and pain for those fleeting snatches of well-being. This is typical of the alcoholic, who honestly believes it is better and more relief-giving to drown his troubles than to face them. This same path is taken by the student who puts off his studies for the quick pleasure of a movie. In the long run the problems of either the alcoholic or the student are compounded. Relief is never lasting if we follow this belief. It is real, but entirely too brief.

IRRATIONAL IDEA NO. 8: *"The idea that one should be dependent on others and needs someone stronger than oneself on whom to rely."*

Excessive dependency stems from two sources: lack of self-confidence and the belief that failure proves one's worthlessness. Relying too much on others tends to perpetuate both conditions. Confidence comes to us only when we have individually accomplished some task. This is learning. One tries, surveys the results, gains from the experience, and tries again. Much learning is trial and error. The trial phase in this process is omitted when others try for us. Therefore, never having attempted a task, our motivation and self-confidence will constantly diminish. Dependency breeds more dependency.

Fear of failure can be avoided by letting others make decisions for us. But this means a loss of freedom and independence, because we must thereafter do what others think is right and ignore our own interests. Worse than the failure we might have incurred is the endless state of frustration we experience because we have turned our lives over to others. Failure is not catastrophic. It is a natural human event that can be of great value in demonstrating to us what ought *not* be attempted at another time. The adage "It is better to have loved and lost than never to have loved at all" is applicable. Only by committing ourselves to a course of action, regardless of the possibility of failure, can we lead truly rewarding lives.

IRRATIONAL IDEA NO. 9: *"The idea that one's past history is an all-important determiner of one's present behavior and that because something once strongly affected one's life, it should indefinitely have a similar effect."*

This philosophy works dangerously against persons in counseling. They erroneously believe that what once existed must always exist, not realizing that experiences that may have shaped the past do not *need* to shape the future. Man is capable of great changes in his personality regardless of past experiences. If he will actively combat his present philosophies, challenge their soundness, and then try a new approach, he may be pleasantly surprised by his degree of success. Only the belief that the past must determine the future is capable of preventing change.

Much of this thinking has entered into society from psychoanalysis and behaviorism, which have repeatedly emphasized the influence of childhood on our adult lives. While these findings cannot be totally refuted, the interpretation that change is impossible unless each childhood memory is revived, must be denied.

This idea is most harmful to those persons who most desperately need help. The female patient who has had several illegitimate births and three failures in marriage, who has been hailed into court for child neglect, probably considers herself as always having been an incorrigible sinner. She is likely to be amused at the assurance that it is perfectly possible for her to lead a sane, well-run life. Her thoughts might be: "Me become a decent person? Are you kidding? I've been a bum all my life. Everything I've ever done proves it. Don't waste your time, doctor. I don't deserve it, and what's more, on a tramp like me it's hopeless. I can't change now. I'll never amount to anything."

We would expect this woman, seeing counseling as a

noble but futile gesture, to leave the office in a hurry. More often than not, she does just that.

IRRATIONAL IDEA NO. 10: *"The idea that one should become quite upset over other people's problems and disturbances."*

On the one hand there is the person, for example, whose every effort is met with tears and laments, such as the adventurous and daring entrepreneur whose wife daily predicts the doom of each of his business ventures. These undisturbed persons tend to resent the additional burden of having to deal with the emotional storms of those close to them, for they already have sufficient pressures to face in simply trying to carry on their affairs. There is also a loss of respect for the hysterical partner who habitually faces each crisis with anguish rather than action.

On the other hand, a second type of person actually uses this human strategy to his advantage. Often he unconsciously counts on the fact that others will be upset over his behavior, thus satisfying his need for attention or revenge. Once they show him their weaknesses by letting him know how mightily they upset themselves over him and under which circumstances they do this, it is reasonably certain this knowledge will be used to his advantage on later occasions. This "game" is played constantly by children and parents. Parents fall into the trap set by their youngsters when they become upset over the children. Thus they unwittingly hurt themselves and satisfy the children's desire for revenge. Husbands and wives also participate frequently in this drama in much the same way that parents and children do. We seem not to realize that the possibility of change in others decreases in direct proportion to the degree of our own loss of emotional control.

We can never change another person's thinking directly. It is always his choice to behave badly if, neurotically, he wishes to. Our demand that he *must* change places us in the role of a dictator or an all-knowing God. Yet he might be right and we might be wrong! Even if we are convinced of our own rightness, the other person still has to be accorded the right to be wrong.

To incur an ulcer or a depression in an attempt to change another individual is folly. Such results are as bad or worse than the disease. Yet, how many women cry when ignored by their husbands? How many husbands explode at the spending habits of their wives? Is being ignored worse than being depressed? Is being furious and perpetually resentful any better than living on a tight budget? The price for change is too great if it entails emotional disturbance, for one disturbance has a way of breeding another until other areas of the relationship are also in jeopardy.

It is far better for the frustrated person to tell himself: "Okay, now calm down. So my wife spends foolishly. No reason to get mad at her, even though I don't like what she's doing. After all, she has lots of wonderful qualities, and if I realize how lucky I am in other ways, I won't get all steamed up over this. She's not perfect, but then neither am I. However, I still don't like this reckless habit of hers. Perhaps I'll have to take over the budget for a while. Or maybe I could give her a separate checking account. If she runs out of money, she'll have to pinch pennies for a time to make it up. Something will probably work. Even if it doesn't, thank God she doesn't have worse habits."

This is a sane, rational approach to a common problem.

This husband will never be facing a wife who is spitefully keeping him in debt because he screams and argues with her.

IRRATIONAL IDEA No. 11: *"The idea that there is invariably a right, precise, and perfect solution to human problems and that it is catastrophic if this perfect solution is not found."*

Only death is certain. To delay a decision because it does not satisfy us totally is a demand for certainty. Normally, problems have several possible solutions, none of which may strike us as ideal. Still, it is far better to initiate *some* action than to take none at all. Yet the latter is what millions of people do constantly. The young lady who rejects suitor after suitor because none is everything she has envisioned, very effectively delivers herself into spinsterhood, loneliness, and depression. Perpetual indecision is far less satisfying than a marriage with a less-than-perfect man might have been.

The inexperienced mother, uncertain of proper discipline for her children, may allow their misconduct to continue until she has found *the* answer for their behavior. She will, of course, wait a long while, during which time the problem itself will grow worse, requiring other "perfect" solutions.

After reasonable thought, the sensible person acts—even if he is uncertain. He is more fearful of inaction than of poor results. He later assesses the results of his decision and arrives at probable answers that will serve him on other occasions. He recognizes that life is not static. What worked extremely well in the past may work no longer. Or that which worked well for one person may not work for another.

Believing it to be catastrophic not to have discovered the ideal solution, the individual further temporarily incapacitates his most important asset in dealing with life's problems: his calm, rational intelligence. After he has become thoroughly overwrought he is probably never going to find a proper solution. Reason and negative emotions cannot operate simultaneously. Either we are thinking clearly (and remain calm) or we are thinking foolishly (and become disturbed). Most persons, in fact, fail to realize that false, inaccurate thinking *is* the negative emotion, and that clear, rational thinking *is* a state of mental calm. We do not think rationally and become calm. Thinking sensibly *is* the calmness itself. And thinking irrationally *is* the disturbance. It is for this reason that we say that reason and disturbance do not coexist. At the same moment one cannot think wisely *and* unwisely.

A Twelfth Irrational Idea

A very troubled young man once sought my help to gain relief from a recent but deep and distressing depression he had been in for the previous two weeks. He related his problem in the first few minutes of the initial session. "I'm wondering if I'm committing adultery. I once belonged to a fundamentalist faith, which I accepted fully and received great comfort from—except for its ruling that I was living in adultery, when it was disclosed that I had remarried. My grounds for divorcing my first wife were not adultery. According to that church, the Bible accepts a divorce as valid only if unfaithfulness has occurred. I left that church years ago and didn't give this matter much thought until I recently heard a revivalist meeting over the radio. Since then I haven't been able to get the thought out of my head that I'm living in deadly sin. Now I'm not sure if I should divorce my wife, leave my children, and live in separation, or remarry my first wife. I'm terrified of God's wrath and the possibility that I'll burn in hell."

My immediate attempt to relieve him of distress was to point out to him that other and fully acceptable religions did not accept this belief of his former church and that comprehension of the Scriptures was often a difference of interpretation. He was aware of this line of thinking, he replied, but it had brought only momentary relief. I next suggested he was blaming himself for possibly living in sin and that even if he accepted the fundamentalist precept, there was still no legitimate reason why he must also hate himself because he was sinning. This argument was intended to make him aware of Irrational Idea No. 2—"The idea that one should be thoroughly competent, adequate, and achieving in all possible respects if one is to consider oneself worthwhile." In his case he was apparently telling himself that if he was not a perfect Christian, he was also not a good and worthwhile human.

As our conversation deepened it was learned that he had grave doubts about Scriptural interpretation as it related to his situation but felt guilty nevertheless. Repeatedly he made reference to the fact that it had to be true because it was stated clearly in the Bible. Still, he could hardly accept the fact that he was a sinner for being married to a loving wife who was doing a conscientious job of rearing his children.

A picture soon emerged of a person who completely submerged his own convictions to those of others. Therefore, it was stressed to him that true belief comes from questioning and arriving at decisions based on one's own examination. He was further urged to study his *own* thoughts on the question of adultery and if he decided that his first church was correct, he ought then to obtain a divorce. If not, he could then live in peace with himself, since his beliefs would have been truly firm and any divergent views would be regarded as erroneous.

During the next several visits his fear of challenging the beliefs of persons he otherwise respected was fully explored until he began to view his present life as a proper one. With this came a marked diminution of his depression.

I was never fully satisfied throughout the course of counseling this client that Irrational Idea No. 2 was ultimately basic to his disturbance. I began to realize that he had a more fundamental irrational notion that forbade him to make an independent judgment over the question of adultery. I saw that his distress was actually caused by two factors: fear of disbelieving what he was told to be gospel truth and guilt for not giving up his second marriage. As I began to understand the dynamics, it seemed that he first had the conviction that he had *no right to question* the authorities who said he was living in adultery; and then, as a consequence of this condition, he blamed himself for being an adulterer. This conviction I would express as

IRRATIONAL IDEA NO. 12: *The idea that beliefs held by respected authorities or society must be correct and should not be questioned.*

Further reflection over this conclusion led me to wonder about the presence of this idea among other people, what its effects are, if any, and how it fits with the eleven irrational ideas stated by Ellis, which we have already cited.

Is this idea not fundamental to the eternal friction between well-meaning parents and their "rebellious" children? This alienation of generations is made more comprehensible when seen as the attempt by adults to deny adolescents the right to question the time-honored standards of the culture. With their fresh and unindoctrinated outlook the youngsters are prone to raise disturbing questions regarding thrift, sexual behavior, obedience to authority, the merits of narcotics, the truths of religion, etc. And is not the adult world constantly retorting: "You must not have such thoughts. Don't be disrespectful." Though an effort is made to give a rationale for the adult beliefs, there is often, nevertheless, a subtle shock response when questions are raised touching emotionally charged or highly valued beliefs. Along with the usual explanations of why there is a God or why one should be chaste until marriage goes the unspoken message: "I'm shocked at the questions you raise. How can you even think of such things?" Over the years the notion is solidly grasped by the child that questioning the dictates of his elders is wrong and that he had better accept them as correct if he is to be assured his security.

Was it not Irrational Idea No. 12 that created the stagnant period of the Middle Ages with its appeal *solely* to Scriptures, its fear of probing science, and its universal reliance on dogma? Was not Nazi Germany a victim of this notion, holding, as it did, that the word of the Fuehrer and his followers was unquestionably true and could not be challenged? Propaganda and brainwashing are applications of the twelfth irrational idea.

The greatest support for postulating a twelfth irrational idea comes from the nature of rational-emotive therapy itself. Emotional disturbance is overcome only after the client has overthrown, through intensive questioning, his fondest illogical beliefs. Unless he challenges the authorities or the society that taught him the first eleven, he cannot change any of them. We have been urging people to reexamine their philosophies, without always realizing that they often felt the philosophies must be correct because respected figures espoused them. We have failed to realize that this, in and of itself, is *another* and more fundamental illogical error that must also be challenged.

The idea is irrational for the following reasons:

1. It presumes that man is capable of perfection, a condition no thinking person can support. Any authority, be it a person or a social institution, has only limited wisdom and through long periods of time often comes to view yesterday's "truths" as today's errors. Wisdom is obtained through the accretion of experience and the erosion of beliefs that do not stand the test of reason. No matter how slowly, practically all beliefs and ideas undergo modification.

2. The very "truths" that the neurotic person fears to question were themselves the product of a previous disbelief. The institution of slavery was once thought of as moral and defensible. Painful and searching inquiry into the justice of this practice eventually modified it into "separate but equal" class distinction. Why should not this modified view also come under scrutiny by the very same process which gave it birth? For the neurotic to avoid the process by which his cherished philosophy was founded is arbitrary and illogical.

3. Deciding which authority or which society a person

will accept is more often an accident of birth, location, and time than it is the result of careful study. "Authoritative" views of widely divergent natures are almost always held by others if one will but explore far enough. To accept one authority is to deny another.

4. Many beliefs are correct only insofar as they are relative. While it may have been "correct" to regard birth control as harmful to a society that was losing many of its members through wars, pestilence, and infant mortality, such a view is no longer tenable in a world threatened with overpopulation. Not only are ideas held through accidents of birth, location, and time, but their truthfulness also seems to be dependent on these accidents. As ethics are now being viewed as situational, so also must the beliefs supporting these ethical positions be viewed as situational.

The secular sciences are increasingly being regarded as valid sources for the faithful as means of living the faith in a more thorough and mature way.[6]

Rather than regard beliefs as eternal truths held by infallible individuals or institutions, a more rational approach would consider these points:

1. Institutions such as governments, universities, and churches are the product of human effort. Since all humans are imperfect and error-prone, so are their institutions. The final truth, therefore, cannot be the province of any person or group of persons.

2. Truth, as scientifically conceived, is always incomplete and is arrived at through controlled trial and error. Each finding is carefully tested to determine the limits of its applicability. For example, normal speeds have no effect upon the size of a moving vehicle or passengers.

This "fact" breaks down, however, as a vehicle approaches the speed of light.

3. Very few thinkers have been able to influence generations long after their deaths. Most respected sages have momentary recognition and are soon forgotten. Since one cannot know how one's mentor will fare in the pages of history, one is wisest always to have reservations about his teachings.

4. Acquaintance with anthropology should be undertaken to impress upon oneself the relativity of belief. As one man's meat is another man's poison, so is one man's belief another man's disbelief.

It is wisest always to ask of oneself: "Why should I believe this?" "What proof is there for that statement?" "What have others to say on this same subject?" "Why is not the opposite true?" Conviction and a saner outlook on life are quite likely to emerge from such intense questioning.

2
The Mechanics of Counseling

IN DISCUSSING THERAPY WITH OTHER COUNSELORS I HAVE often benefited most from direct suggestions about procedure rather than from theory. The novice is especially hungry for such details, and as a foundation for counseling he should have the benefit of all the shortcuts and working techniques it has taken others years of practice to acquire. Such simple questions as: "Must I keep a client a full hour? Should I counsel him only in my office? Can I start the hour by talking about the weather? Is it all right to recommend a book? What's the best way to end a counseling session?" are perfectly legitimate. For what my experience is worth, I share the following.

Time and Place

For most counseling to be efficient, especially if it is long-term, privacy in a soundproof room is very important. The average time per session varies between thirty and fifty minutes. This permits the counselor a short break of ten to fifteen minutes before his next appointment, during which time he can make phone calls and notes, or just rise and stretch. The office of the pastor is far preferable to the client's home, since it prohibits the constant intrusion of children, phone calls, or salesmen. When continued counseling has been agreed upon, it is vastly simpler for the client to go to the minister's office than for him to call at the various homes of his clients. Clients quickly accustom themselves to the schedule, and the women in particular enjoy the opportunity to dress up and get out of the home. If the pastor can have a reception room with a few small chairs and a small desk or table, crayons, paper, and comics, even the children can be brought along, thus making attendance at her appointment more attractive for the mother.

The office needs only a few chairs. A desk is desirable but only as a place to administer the pastor's affairs. It is unnecessary for counseling. Whether the client sits alongside of, or in front of the desk, is immaterial. Quiet and reasonable comfort are more important than decor.

This description of the usual locale should not deter a minister from counseling in less orthodox places. It can readily be seen that the type of conversation encountered in RET can be carried on profitably almost anywhere and at almost any time. I have imparted the principles of a sound emotional life in diverse places and on various spontaneous occasions. I have counseled over a cup of coffee in the corner café with a car salesman, at home when an acquaintance simply dropped in to chat, or at a meal, with a couple with whom my wife and I were dining. If someone asks me why he was upset over an event, I do not hesitate (assuming it would be keeping within the bounds of good taste) to discuss how the event cannot upset him and how his opinions instead were the cause. I would do this with children in the neighborhood or with my own. Reason is no stranger to time and place. When the opportunity exists the counselor can at least start to get the other person to change his thinking.

The minister has ample time and opportunity to influence the neurotic habits of his congregation. The Sunday service is, of course, an excellent opportunity. His hospital and home visits afford a multitude of chances to help the mentally distressed.

"What!" you may protest. "Throw logic and reason at my people while I am making a social visit?"

Yes, why not? What is wrong with helping an angry mother who tells us as she sets her table for our visit that her son is driving her to distraction? You and she may normally pray openly for divine help, but is it not true that any conversation designed to bring about good could also be called prayer? Why not show her that her anger, which she could control if she understood the ABC's of emotion, is encouraging the boy's misconduct, is doing great damage to herself, and is making matters worse? If she is alone, counseling could proceed immediately.

I compare such conversations with those one has with a neighbor when advising him on the care of his lawn or with the mechanic when he is explaining the necessity of a brake relining job. Both will point out the reason and logic of their advice and possibly document it with personal experience. And have we not often learned from such brief encounters?

Opening the Session

When possible, get to the point with such questions as: "How can I help you? What's on your mind? What's troubling you? What would you care to talk about today?" This establishes very quickly the give-and-take relationship that you will be practicing during the hour. You will give of your knowledge, and (you hope) he will take of it. You will then listen to his complaints while trying to get a picture of his disturbance. Interrupt and ask questions when you are confused. Then ask him to continue. If he veers too far from the major issues, pull him back with a comment such as: "That's all very interesting, and I'd like to hear more about it later. For now, however, I'm more curious about what happened after she said she'd leave you (or whatever the point of interest might be)." The counselor is in charge in this relationship and should not hesitate to direct the talk along meaningful lines.

When a client has great difficulty speaking, it is far better to carry on a monologue than to sit in silence for more than a minute or two. The pastor can sympathetically assure the client that his aversion against revealing his personal problems is natural, but that through experience he, the pastor, has heard just about all the tragic and embarrassing stories that can be told. If reasonable warmth does not break the wall of silence, the pastor will want to tempt the client into a conversation by challenging him with fresh ideas, such as are abundant in RET, until the client cannot leave them unquestioned. Suppose a woman, after unsuccessfully being urged to continue, says, "My husband . . ." and begins sobbing. Unless she is able to resume in reasonable time, the pastor can proceed: "I don't know what the problem is with your husband, and I'm eager to find out. However, whatever it is, I must point out to you that nothing he has done is actually upsetting you. He's not even here with us now and you're upset. You're really upsetting yourself and I'd like to show you how you are doing it." Then an explanation of the ABC's of the emotions could be offered. This usually brings on questions and even protests. At least she will be talking. If not, continue along in a calm manner, lecturing, if you will, about the principles of emotional control.

Another assault on such resistances will be your acceptance of her silence with assurances that you understand how she is struggling with being candid and that you will gladly wait until she is ready to speak. If this brings no response, the reality of the situation will have to be made very clear to her. "I'm sorry you don't want to talk about your problems, Mrs. Quill, but I cannot help you unless you tell me what's wrong."

It is extremely rare that one or the other of these techniques does not break the fear and start a flow of conversation. If the minister remains calm (and why shouldn't he, since she is not upsetting him), she will see his kindness and perhaps want to return. I have had numerous people begin with such a resistance, but each was eventually put at ease in several sessions.

When a client opens the session with a comment about the latest model cars or the baseball scores, I do not hesitate to join in. This may sometimes go on for five minutes. Usually, before that much time has elapsed, he has himself directed the conversation to the business of counseling. If not, I simply suggest: "Yes, I'd like to have a car like that too. Well, now, what can I do for you? What's the problem?" And so we proceed.

When a counselor forgets what the client spoke of during the previous session, it is best to open the hour with a question such as, "Have you been thinking over what we talked about last time?" His response will usually bring recall. Or one might also try: "Now let's see what you learned from your last visit. What did we talk about?" Usually the client will summarize enough for us to recall that hour and his particular problem. Should none of these work, it is best to be honest and state: "I'm terribly sorry I've forgotten what your problem was. I've seen a number of people in the meantime and I sometimes forget. Could you brush me up on it briefly?" The minister need feel no embarrassment for such slips of memory. After all, he too is human.

What to Look for and Talk About

With a new client it is essential to get an impression of his problem as soon as possible. This can take five minutes or most of the hour. It should rarely take longer. I know that other therapists request lengthy histories and elaborate testing, and that they allow the subject to explain his circumstances for hours before actively intervening. This is a regrettable practice. It is time-consuming, allowing the client to suffer needlessly while he is being processed and evaluated. Why does he have to be evaluated? Why does he even need to be diagnosed? Will it make any difference in what we do? In most cases it will not, but there are a few exceptions.

When the pastoral counselor suspects that he is dealing with a problem beyond his competence, he should not hesitate to seek expert assistance. In such instances, extended diagnostic studies definitely do have a place in counseling. Sometimes the question of mental retardation arises. This can usually be easily determined by referring the client to a psychologist for intelligence testing. Sometimes the client may be psychotic or on the border between psychosis and neurosis. Some psychotic states are not easily detected, such as the paranoid. Referral to a psychologist, psychiatrist, or psychiatric social worker is certainly recommended, because such clients are additionally difficult to understand and help. Should the minister suspect that his client has pronounced suicidal intentions, he should at once refer him to someone in the mental health profession. Unless he is quite adept at helping the client over his guilt or resentment, he should not undertake for long to counsel this person. This has particular importance in pastoral counseling because of its frequent emphasis on sin and guilt, the very factors usually creating the wish for death. In the hands of a condemning minister, the depressed client is a prime candidate for the act of suicide.

And lastly, when physical complaints are part of the syndrome, the wise counselor refers the subject to a physician. If a physical cause is discovered, the minister has saved himself a great deal of time and does a great service for the client. If the physical findings are negative, he can then resume his counseling with the assurance that the physical pains result from tensions and may be eased through counseling.

Assuming then that our client is not terribly disturbed or does not fall into one of the categories mentioned above, we can, without further fanfare, proceed to show him through reason why all of the nonsense that he believes to be true is not true, whether we regard him as being in an anxiety state, or as a depressive, or as a psychopath. Therefore, instead of using lengthy work-up procedures, we attempt to have the client discuss his problems immediately. As he does he will very easily reveal his belief in certain irrational ideas. As these occur, mental notes are made of them until we decide which idea is causing the greatest disturbance. That idea should be challenged first. Sometimes this decision can be made quickly; at other times it requires patient study. In almost all cases the counselor should, within the first hour, have identified the major irrational idea and explained it to the subject as well. Normally a first hour of rational-emotive counseling that does not accomplish this is a failure.

Let us take the case of Mr. Bridge, who opened his hour with: "Doctor Hauck, it's my wife. I wish you could do something for her. She makes me so unhappy and guilty about my work I can't concentrate. I'm trying my best to organize a political party in this city, and for the life of me I won't be able to do it if she doesn't stop her griping. She gets depressed about being left alone evenings and when I come home lashes out at me until we wind up arguing until two in the morning. Lately I've been drinking a bit heavy just trying to forget her. Something has to be done. She's got to be made to realize that I must accomplish this goal. Our party hasn't won an election in this place in fifty years and this has to stop."

With no more than this, the counselor is ready to start. In fact, he has three starting points and ought to consider which to focus on first. The counselor could challenge one of the following notions: (*a*) that Mr. Bridge's wife is upsetting him; (*b*) that he is upsetting his wife; and (*c*) that he must organize a political party. Each of these would offer a good beginning, but the third issue is probably the best to focus on first.

If he can be made to reduce the size of his ambition, his wife's nagging will automatically be lessened, and thus his guilt and resentment will also be relieved. If, on the other hand, his belief that he is upsetting her is immediately challenged, he may proceed even more actively on his course but experience less guilt and unhappiness. He would, it is true, benefit by accomplishing his goal, but the relationship between him and his wife would deteriorate. Unless she too could be seen in counseling (either separately or with her husband), she could tend to become more neurotic. A similar state might occur if he were shown that she is not upsetting him, only frustrating him.

We should proceed, therefore, by challenging the idea that he *must* achieve his goal—a strong political party for his city. He would be shown that he has convinced himself of having a *need* rather than a strong *wish*. For example, his city has not needed his party for years and it can very well continue without it. Wanting to create an opposition group might be quite sound politically, but how does this prove the city *must* have a sound political climate? How much will society really benefit by his hard work, even if he succeeds? If he insists that it is truly greatly needed and would correct a great many social evils, we may have to concede him his point and give attention to his wife to get her to accept his project. Usually such urgency cannot be demonstrated. We could then ask him to weigh his gains as a political organizer against his inevitable losses at home. As desirable as a new party might be, that is still no argument that it must be created or that it is essential that he be the one to organize it.

We would engage this man in counseling quite actively after this brief explanation. He has clearly stated his difficulty and given us much to work on. In a fraction of the session's time we would have identified at least three of the irrational ideas that he is suffering from and we would be making him think seriously about one of them. The three irrational ideas are: No. 4—"The idea that it is awful and catastrophic when things are not the way one would very much like them to be"; No. 5—"the idea that human unhappiness is externally caused and that people have little or no ability to control their sorrows and disturbances"; and No. 10—"the idea that one should become quite upset over other people's problems and disturbances."

RET guides itself a great deal by the material offered by the client. If the client informs us that he is upset over being unemployed, we see no reason normally why such a statement should not be accepted at face value. The counselor, however, is cautioned always to hold some suspicion in reserve and not to hesitate to look beyond an explanation offered by the client. Often enough, the subject may deny the truth or know it but believe it is unimportant. Should the counselor work only on the statements made by the parishioner, he can be led to focus on issues that are irrelevant or of only secondary importance.

A high school boy who counseled with me concerning his social awkwardness started out the third session by saying, "I don't think I'll be coming to therapy after today."

I naturally asked him why he wanted to terminate, and he replied that he felt he must learn independence. Only by leaving counseling and pulling himself up by his own bootstraps, he felt, could he develop the necessary feelings of self-confidence to break his dependency patterns.

This sounded like a valid concern to me, so I immediately entered into a long discourse to show him that my efforts would never encourage undue dependence upon me. Though he might for the present need me to show him how to gain self-confidence, he could rest assured that I would be only too willing to welcome his growth.

He returned for another appointment but only to repeat his desire to make this his last visit. On hearing this I concluded that he still needlessly feared becoming dependent on me or that he wanted to leave counseling for an entirely different reason.

This is a crucial point, for unless we grant an alternate reason, we may endlessly debate with each other over a dead issue.

"What else might you be telling yourself about wanting to end counseling?" I said.

"Nothing, really. I just feel I should learn to do for myself and that if I keep on coming back to you each week, I'll be doing the same old thing I've always done."

"Then you don't believe me when I say I want to teach you how to break your dependency leanings?"

"Actually I do. But I still have a strong feeling I should not come back."

"Maybe your reason for wanting to terminate has nothing to do with the fear of becoming dependent. What else do you think you're telling yourself about counseling?"

"What else? Gee, I don't know, unless it could be that I don't want anyone to know I'm coming here."

Here was an explanation that seemed valid. It too was pursued and shown to be illogical. This time, however, his resistance was removed and we continued on for several months of productive work.

The Use of Authority

The counselor is not God. This does not, however, forbid or rule out his right and duty to speak from authority when his training and experience convince him he is correct. If an issue arises with which he cannot agree, he ought to speak out against it clearly and forcefully. If the result is a discussion over the issue, this is fine. No one is converted to a belief until he has raised all possible objections to it. The more confrontation offered against his neurotic beliefs, the sooner the neurotic will be under a mental pressure to reexamine his favorite notions and eventually to replace them with rational beliefs.

Most therapies have advised a soft approach to this matter of changing another person's opinions. If by soft and gentle we mean tactful, considerate, and undictatorial, I approve. If by a soft approach we mean to persuade by disagreeing slightly with the other person's philosophy or by approaching the subject obliquely, I cannot agree. It has never hurt any client to have his beliefs questioned. If he is certain of himself, he will quickly discard other views with no damage to himself. If he is uncertain and slightly open to suggestion, the voice of authority needs to be loud to be heard at all.

A young man once complained to me: "I don't think I'm getting anywhere, doctor. This counseling is taking so long and I don't see any improvement."

"Wait a minute, Tom," I protested, "there you go again, being the same old defeatist again. What do you mean, you haven't progressed? Just last week you told me about how you finally stood up to that bully brother of yours. And look at how you've been doing at school. You're volunteering answers in class, mixing better with your classmates, and even dating a little."

"Yes, I know. But I began that quite a while ago. Look what happened this week."

"So this week you let your friend talk you out of some money. So what? You can't make steady progress each week. You're bound to slip back once in a while, don't you think?"

"I suppose so, but I really shouldn't . . ."

"You suppose nothing. Stop giving yourself a rough

time because you weren't perfect. You're doing fine and you know it. Just stop and think how well you would have thought you were doing if I had told you before we started working together that you'd accomplish what you did. You'd have thought that was real progress wouldn't you?"

"Yes, I'm sure I would have," he said.

"Well then, is it less progress now that you've done it?"

Through such a judicious use of authority, the counselor, in the role of instructor, gives unmistakable evidence to the student that he is wrong and explains why. He does not allow the young man to view his actual gains as lucky breaks or insignificant steps toward greater improvement. Many clients are too quick to feel discouragement at the occasional slow pace of improvement, and this habit must be actively combatted by the knowing and perhaps stern voice of the "expert" who is saying, "It is not so."

The opposite behavior is sometimes experienced in counseling. This may require the same bluntness to make the client stop resting on his successes. Mr. Sitter, an insurance agent, was troubled with falling sales. Consequently he began finding it ever more difficult to knock on strange doors. He would rationalize that the people were probably not at home, or not in need of insurance, or had no money, etc. After convincing him that he was doing things the "hard" way while he thought he was taking the "easy" way out, I assigned him the task of calling on every person whose name appeared in his schedule, but whom he had never called upon.

One day I asked, "How many customers on your list did you visit this week?"

"I was really too busy seeing my regular policyholders this week to find the time to visit new clients."

"You mean you didn't knock on one strange door all week?"

"I had plenty to do with taking care of my regular people. Really, I'm not making an excuse."

"Perhaps not, but I get the distinct feeling you're trying to pull the wool over your own eyes."

"No, I'm not. I know you advised me to make at least one new contact every day. I understand that, but this week I couldn't."

"Please don't apologize to me. You're the one with the poor sales record. If it doesn't bother you, fine. But such is not the case. You aren't happy about your success as an insurance man and one of the reasons for that is your fear to make new contacts. We know why you have the fear. Now you have to practice knocking on doors to overcome it. And that, Mr. Sitter, is exactly where you're falling down on the job. You make one fine excuse after the other. Last week you saw two new people. The rest of the time you were sick, or visiting relatives, or something. You'll never get used to talking to strangers at this rate. You're goofing off badly and you might as well admit it."

If this degree of pressure does not push the client toward greater action, the pressure should be increased. Suppose this procrastinator still works halfheartedly at his problem over the next several weeks. He might then have to be approached in this manner: "Mr. Sitter, you're certainly asking for misery. Your living depends on making new contacts and you won't make them. You're still stupidly telling yourself it is less painful to starve than it is to be turned away by a disinterested person. How foolish can you be? You have enough intelligence to know that's not so, yet that's what you actually believe. Come on now.

Do what you have to do, whether you like it or not, and stop acting like a dunce."

This may seem like strong language that the client would refuse to listen to. On the contrary, if we are being candid for his own good, we can say such things and have them accepted. It is essential to remember one technique, however, if such candor is to be used: the counselor must be honestly in sympathy with the client. He must like the client even though the latter stalls and repeats his neurotic behavior. The counselor must separate in his own mind the man's behavior from the man himself. It is what the client is *doing*, not the client himself, that the minister attacks. If this feeling is clearly conveyed, it is amazing how direct one can be with others without their taking offense. I have made comments to clients such as: "You're a real doormat." "You were really a coward when you would not talk back." "If you don't make your children do what you tell them, they will think you're nothing but a big bag of wind."

These kinds of frank statements can safely be made, and should be made, to break the client's natural inertia—provided he does not feel that *he* is under personal attack.

Interruptions

Phone calls, a knock on the office door, or just the wish to make a note to bring home a loaf of bread are among the normal interruptions every counselor encounters. In the past we have been cautioned never to allow anyone or anything to invade the sacred privacy of the counseling hour. This is fine if it can always be carried out without causing too much inconvenience to the counselor. But phone calls *can* be accepted during the therapy hour and the caller advised to call back. A knock on the door can also be answered with a brief comment that we will tend to the matter shortly. As long as such interruptions are not the rule they need cause no concern. Even if the subject has to be left alone in the office a few minutes, he could be thinking over our previous remarks to good advantage.

The Counselor as Model

During counseling of the RET variety the client is confronted with a number of strange and almost outlandish notions that he simply cannot accept without serious doubt. We tell him that emotional reactions are never created by anyone but oneself, that no one should ever be blamed for anything, or that it is better to do than to do well. Such notions are so at variance with the usual outlook that vivid proof of their being true is sometimes needed in order to overcome the initial skepticism that is certain to arise. If he can be persuaded to employ rational principles and then has some measure of success, the client will soon enough see how right the counselor has been. The next best proof, however, is to see how these principles of emotional control work for the counselor. The client who asks in disbelief, "Do you really mean that nothing should ever upset me?" can be answered with: "Of course I mean that. I haven't been disturbed once in the past three years. And I don't suppose my problems have been any worse than yours. I just think about them differently, so I feel differently about them too."

When the client asks how to handle this or that problem, the counselor ought to give personal testimony from his own life if he has a satisfactory experience to offer as an example. A male with whom I had spent several sessions teaching control over worrying, claimed he was finding it very difficult to put my advice into practice. I decided to show him how I had done it on one occasion months before.

"I remember having an uneasy feeling of tension in my stomach one morning and wondered what was wrong. I knew, of course, that I was upsetting myself over something, so I proceeded to look into my mind to find out what I was telling myself. At first I didn't have much success. I thought of my job, and it didn't seem to be that. I thought of the family, but everything had gone well in that department. I kept thinking of what might be troubling me. Finally, after about fifteen minutes of this soul-searching I realized I was worried that I might lose a good friend because of a heated discussion we had on politics a week before. A few days after this talk he begged off on a trip we had planned and I wondered if he had taken our debate more seriously than I realized.

"Ordinarily it only takes me a moment to locate the thoughts that are troubling me, but on this occasion I needed much longer, and I knew I would have to stick with it and find them or I'd be mildly tense all day. Once I located the irrational idea—that it would be a catastrophe to lose his friendship—I questioned and challenged it for another forty-five minutes until I had convinced myself it would be regrettable to lose him but hardly the life or death matter that I was making it.

"As I say, this whole process took me an hour before I was completely back to normal. That's a long time for me. For you, it might take all day at first. If so, take all day. You will get better, the more you try."

Confidence is gained very rapidly when a client knows

he is talking to someone who has had firsthand knowledge of his dilemma and has conquered it. This, of course, puts a burden on the counselor. He cannot be very effective in helping others if he is often irrational himself. Many counseling failures can be attributed to counselors who could not follow their own sound advice.

Whom to Believe

An annoyance to many pastors seems to be the dilemma of getting one set of facts from, let us say, the husband, and a contradictory set of facts from the wife. The minister may spend much unnecessary time tracking down the truth of their statements, only to find that he has alienated himself from the spouse he disagreed with. When Mrs. Brown complains that her husband is unreasonable in his drinking, and Mr. Brown insists that he has only "a couple of beers each night with the boys," it matters little whether we discover the "truth." In these cases each person is probably telling the truth as he or she sees it.

It is much wiser to accept *each* set of facts as being true and then to pose the question, "Assuming your husband drinks as much as you say, Mrs. Brown, what do you plan to do about it and why are you upset over it?"

To the husband one could post a similar query: "Your wife describes you as an alcoholic. You say she is exaggerating. Okay, let's just say she is. What can you do about her making a mountain out of a couple of beers instead of arguing with her all the time?"

These questions can be asked of each in separate sessions or even in front of each other if both are seen together. This further avoids the counselor having to take sides. More accurately, he takes *both* sides. He is accepting reality as each person gives it to him and he encourages them to work and live within that reality if it cannot be changed.

Mrs. Alton complained that her husband did not have to be as late for dinner as he often was. Mr. Alton insisted that he could not leave the office at an exact time. Important last-minute details always came up. The minister, even if he knows the couple well and thinks perhaps Mrs. Alton is right, should forget his opinion and accept each party's story at face value. He will have more success if he explains to each how they are neurotically upsetting themselves over the other's behavior, and how their time would be better spent trying to solve the problem. Mrs. Alton might be advised to prepare sumptuous meals that her husband would find difficult to resist. She might refuse to cook a separate meal late in the evening, giving him the warmed-up six o'clock meal. If she chose, she might refuse to cook suppers entirely and might take the family out to dinner a few nights following her husband's unreasonable tardiness. If no plan worked, she might simply have to accept the situation calmly and philosophically. With proper thinking this could be done. She would have to be instructed to challenge such thoughts as: "How unfair of him. How can he do this to me? What a louse I have for a husband. I'll show him." And she would have to be instructed to think along rational lines such as: "So I feed him at eight every night. I don't like it, but that's hardly worth breaking our marriage over. Even though it is extra work, it won't kill me. After all, he's working late for our benefit. Since I can't make him change, I'll just have to go along with him."

The husband would have to be retrained along similar lines. When the irrationalities of both are worked on, it is a rare marriage that does not improve. It may not be idyllic, but some improvement is better than none.

Bibliotherapy

Reason does not make itself known only through the spoken word. The written word has sometimes succeeded where speech has failed. A book has the advantage of being available when the client cares to study it. He can go over a passage as often as he likes, at his own pace—something not always possible in verbal therapy. He can find confirmation in other writers who express themselves better for his purposes than his counselor might do.

Bibliotherapy is a time-honored method among the clergy. Their greatest source of guidance has been the Bible. In addition, however, the minister should not hesitate to advise the reading of books he has found especially useful. He may at the same time mention what, in his opinion, are a book's strong and weak points, thereby avoiding some future confusion.

On more than one occasion I have advised the study of history, hoping to demonstrate to the client how much suffering other people in the world have had to endure and how they accepted their plights with little complaint. A father who feels badly that his earnings are temporarily insufficient to provide meat on the table each day could profitably study the library copy of Will Durant's *Caesar and Christ* from *The Story of Civilization.*[7] There he would find that the mighty Roman army was almost exclusively vegetarian, that most of the world throughout history has considered meat a luxury, and that India has for centuries had millions of its people practice voluntary vegetarianism.

The husband whose marriage does not offer enough sexual satisfaction would be well advised to read about the lives of the saints. He will be hard pressed to feel too sorry for himself when he learns of the fantastic suffering some men have been able to endure gladly and willingly.

To assist him in getting his reasoning across to the client, the counselor may advise the student to read any of the usual textbooks on good mental health, particularly those dealing with the use of reason such as Ellis' *How to Live with a Neurotic*,[8] Ellis and Harper's *A Guide to Rational Living*,[9] or Hauck's *The Rational Management of Children*.[10] Each minister will have his favorites to recommend and should never hesitate to do so if the client is the studious type.

How to Win Friends and Influence People,[11] by Dale Carnegie, embodies many sound principles and has often been recommended by me to my clients. Though I could not wholeheartedly recommend *The Power of Positive Thinking*,[12] by Peale, I have referred the conservatively oriented fundamentalist to it if he could not accept the fact that his thinking, not his environment, disturbed him. Presently the book market seems to be swamped with inspirational material, some of which gives excellent advice on how to overcome one's obstacles.

Dreams and the Transference Phenomenon

Ministers trained along orthodox Freudian or neo-Freudian lines will be attuned to the subject's dreams and his neurotic feelings for the counselor. How does RET handle these? They are not ignored. Nor are they analyzed in depth. They too may represent irrational ideas and as such are dealt with as any other irrational material is managed. If a patient reports waking up from a nightmare in which her father was chasing her with an ax, we will point out how she is "catastrophizing" about her father, how she no longer has to fear him as before, and that she ought to assert her independence of him.

If she evidences the same fear of disapproval by the counselor as she had for her father, this too can be reasoned with. She can be encouraged to see that the counselor's disapproval is unlikely—or, if true, is not harmful. When this happened recently, I had the following conversation:

"It seems you're afraid to confide in me anymore because I might become angry over your behavior as your father was. Stop and think now, Mrs. Thomas. What harm could I really do to you if I didn't like what you're afraid to talk about?"

"You could refuse to see me again," was her instant reply.

"True, I could. Do you think I'd really do that?"

"No, I suppose not, if I want to be really honest about it. But I'm sure you wouldn't like me anymore."

"I hear a lot of things, Mrs. Thomas, and I doubt that you could tell me anything shocking. But let's suppose I did become disenchanted with you. So what?"

"I couldn't stand that. You're the only one I can talk to and I'm afraid you wouldn't want to see me anymore if I told you everything."

"Why couldn't you stand being rejected by me? If I wouldn't like what you've done and I want to get neurotic about it, that's *my* problem, not yours. Sure, you wouldn't want me to dislike you, but it would hardly be terrible if you had to see another counselor, would it?"

"I don't think I could stand it."

"But suppose I moved or died. What would you do then?"

Notice how little attention is paid to her father. We do not take her back into the past needlessly. It might be important to show her how this habit pattern worked with her father, but only insofar as it demonstrates how repetitive and inappropriate her neurotic ideas are today.

The Counselor Plays God

One of the surest ways to defeat oneself as a counselor is to believe that one must perform great feats with each and every client. This is a two-edged sword. It acts on the counselor and the client in very different ways.

The counselor who blames himself for achieving little or no success will undermine his trust in himself. When he counsels again he will unconsciously try to cancel out his previous defeat by making his next counseling endeavor a resounding success. He will then find himself pushing too hard or losing sight of his goals until the client senses the strain to live up to the counselor's expectations. This can be very unnerving to the client—the thought that the pastor's well-being depends on *him*. He already is beset with problems and blames himself for numerous failures. Asking him to be that miraculous "cure" which we all desire is a heavy burden for him and will bring on swift guilt when he falls short of our expectations.

Like a surgeon who detaches himself emotionally from the pain he daily works with, so too must the counselor separate himself from the suffering of his clients if he wants to be of help. The neurotic client does not respect the equally neurotic counselor. Though he may think us unfeeling when we show little sympathy for his unfair treatment by his employer, or when we calmly wait for a female patient to stop sobbing, the fact that we have maintained our calm is reassuring to such a person. We have set an example of how one can control one's feelings. If he or she ever had doubts as to the validity of our recommendations, the client can now verify their efficacy.

More important than this, however, is the fact that when the counselor does not care too much whether a person improves, this has the effect of placing the problem squarely on the client, where it belongs. Only the client can really change himself. No amount of wishing or doing on our part can bring this about unless he is willing to use our help. If we too eagerly want a good life for him, he can reverse the situation and deliberately try to frustrate us. This is stupid and neurotic on his part, but as Ellis has said, "A neurotic is a non-stupid person who behaves stupidly." It is far better to counsel from a distance, always offering people our best, but informing them that it will neither make us ecstatic if they improve nor depress us if they fail. We must always be unassailable emotionally. Knowing this, clients will ignore us somewhat and occupy themselves with their own lives.

A young woman who was making herself very unhappy over her financial situation, blamed herself exceedingly for not being able to offer a more presentable home to friends and relatives.

"Mrs. Wilton, I've told you a dozen times already how it is not your house that makes you unhappy, but your thinking about the house. Still you keep insisting that you have nothing to do with your miserable feelings."

"I just can't tell myself those things you advise. I try to talk myself out of feeling so awful, but it doesn't work."

"You mean you *won't* talk yourself out of them. You see

as well as I do that your run-down house wouldn't bother you a bit if everyone else's house were worse. So every time you feel sorry for yourself over your situation you could fight it by reminding yourself of that. Instead, you keep on believing your house is a reflection of you. Unless you fight it harder than you have been doing, you're going to be miserable for the rest of your life, or until you can get a grand house. If that's what you want, be my guest."

"You needn't say it that way, doctor. I'm trying my best to please you."

"I know you are, and that's half of your problem. Forget about me and please yourself for a change. For your sake I'd like to see you change and become a less disturbed person. Whether you do or not, however, is not critical with me. You're the one who's suffering, not me. If you don't care how often you tie yourself up into emotional knots, why should I? This is your struggle and no one else's. All I can do is to show you how to live better. You must do the work."

Such candor is refreshing for most clients. They see the inevitability of their taking personal responsibility in counseling. They may complain, cry, or pity themselves, but unless they act responsibly they will find themselves impaled upon a shaft of lassitude.

This approach may be uncomfortable for ministers who, often through habit, assume moralistic attitudes. They are prone to say, "But you *can't* go on getting into trouble with the law," when they would do better to say, "It may be hard for you to watch your speed, but unless you force yourself to drive sensibly I suppose I can spare some time to visit you in jail."

This is what is meant by not taking their problems too

seriously. We do not want individuals to be hurt. But if they are determined in their resistance, we can often change their minds by showing them that this attitude means no one will suffer as much as they. We do not have godly powers, and we must anticipate that our clients will move contrary to our best advice. We need not be upset over this. It is the client's problem and he has every right to keep it if he so chooses.

Closing the Hour

There are several standard techniques that are excellent for closing a session. One should not be used to the exclusion of the others, but that technique should be selected which is most appropriate to the need.

1. When the counselor sees that the hour is drawing to a close, he should end his remarks or let the client finish making his point, and then he should say: "Our time is about up now. See you at this same hour next week." If this was the first hour and the client has not yet agreed to continue in counseling, that point should now be clarified.

"Our time is about up, Mr. Jones. I'm sorry we couldn't answer all your questions today, so I think you should come back again—maybe even a number of times—so I can continue to show you how you've been upsetting yourself and what you can do in each case to avoid this in the future. Do you think you could come back next Thursday at one o'clock?"

2. At times it is very important to bolster the client's flagging confidence in himself. He may have been seeing the counselor for several sessions and may now be disappointed that his ten-year-old problem is not removed in

three weeks. Encouragement and praise as the final notes of the hour can often motivate him enough to return again and to work hard on his problem in the meantime.

"Okay, that's about all for today. Before we have the next appointment though, I'd like to compliment you again on how well you did this week. Sure, you fumbled around somewhat, but that's par for the course. Don't get discouraged. You won't master all of this new thinking in a few weeks. If you keep trying, however, you'll eventually have more and more success until these new habits completely replace the old ones. Keep up the good work and I'll see you Wednesday."

Reassurance that he is not wasting his time or that he is not doing worse than other clients, can lift his spirits enough to have him stay with the task. Praising the client (even when he has failed, he can be praised for having tried) is emotional nourishment that the counselor has in ever-ready abundance. Praise, rather than blame, is the food on which clients survive counseling.

3. A rational hour brings forth ideas totally foreign to many people. Not only is it difficult for them to accept the ideas at once, but the several new lines of thought that they must learn concurrently can be confusing. To assess how much has been digested, it behooves the pastor to ask: "I've given you a lot to think about in this hour, and I want to see if you have understood it all. Would you please summarize for me some of the most important points I've made?" This is a test to see how successful we have been. If he repeats only a fraction of the lesson, this is the time to review the other points quickly and to correct any glaring misconceptions.

"And don't forget what we said about being firm with your boy. Remember, if you don't sit down on him now, he'll soon be so big you won't be able to do it at all. And one thing more. I didn't say it was unhealthy to try to be the best mother on the street. You should try very hard to be the best you can be. I only meant that it is not *necessary* to be the greatest mother. Don't confuse healthy wishes with sick needs. Can you remember that point? Fine, see you next week."

4. Homework assignments are important to eventual change. The period before the close of the hour is usually a fine time to discuss them. If the client protests he cannot carry out the assignment the next week, this is the time to question and make other plans.

"Before closing, Mr. Reston, I want to give you a specific assignment. During the next week I want you to go out of your way to do something especially nice for your wife. Buy her a box of candy one day, take her to a movie the next, and so on. Do something nice each day."

"Sorry, doctor, I just remembered this week my wife is visiting her folks and taking the two smallest kids with her."

"All right then, carry out the same assignment with your oldest child. You haven't always gotten along real well with her, have you? Or, if that's impractical, do it with a neighbor or someone at work. Come to think of it, you could still do a good turn for your wife even though she's gone. Can't you call her a couple of times, or send her a gift or a nice letter, or finish painting that bedroom she's been bothering you about?"

"I see your point. Okay, I'll try."

"Fine, and if you will, I'd like you to make a note of what you did each day so we can discuss it in detail when you come next week. See you then, same time."

3
Modifying Behavior Through RET

IN THE PAGES THAT FOLLOW, THE READER WILL PERHAPS gain the impression that rational-emotive therapy is unfeeling, cold, and unheedful of the emotional stress that the client is suffering. In a later chapter we will attempt to show the technique by which the apparent sting of reason is mitigated by emotional rapport. Unfortunately, the written word cannot carry the warm and often humorous inflections that a trained RET counselor employs. It should, therefore, be borne constantly in mind that the samples of counseling that follow are not given in the tone they quite naturally take on when seen in written form. For instance, though the client is frequently disagreed with and a heated debate may arise over an issue, the pastor must always remember that these interchanges, to be therapeutic, are never offered vindictively or sarcastically. The client's right to hold to his belief is accepted as inviolable. The client is always seen as an individual who is whole, whose situation must be assessed in its totality, and who can never be browbeaten or shamed into compliance.

This note of caution is especially important for the clergyman who tends to separate the approaches of reason and emotion. Some become so abstract and philosophical as to become obscure. Others are so impassioned as to offer no logical basis for accepting their thoughts.

Only if this caution is constantly brought to mind can this material be accurately interpreted. Having said this, we may turn our attention to the process of modifying behavior through RET.

To accomplish change in neurotic behavior using rational-emotive psychotherapy, a three-step process must be followed. (1) The irrational idea or ideas must be identified. (2) These ideas must be challenged until disbelieved. (3) New habit patterns must be attempted.

1. Identifying the Irrational Idea

Sometimes a client realizes immediately that he has been talking nonsense to himself. When it is the counselor's good fortune to have such a client, the task of identifying the irrational ideas is rather simple. We simply ask him to tell us what he was thinking *before* he felt disturbed. We then proceed to show him how that thought or thoughts created the consequent feelings.

Often, however, the client will insist that he did not have any thoughts that he was telling himself. This must be vigorously refuted. It must be pointed out to him that thinking is going on continually, even during sleep (in the form of dreams) and that he had to have been thinking something before he felt tense. The subject must then be convinced, through instruction, of the ABC theory of emotions. Since thinking always precedes emotions, he must look closer for those thoughts in the future. In most cases when the client continues to be unable to identify his thoughts, the counselor can suggest what was probably going on in his mind at the time. Common sense and knowledge of the irrational ideas are excellent guides in enabling the counselor to guess the nature of these thoughts.

Mrs. Stockton reported being very nervous one night after her husband returned home from work. She did not have the slightest idea why she felt tense, remembering nothing that would have so affected her. When I then asked what she had done that day it was revealed that she had bought a new dress that cost more than she could afford. Her husband was a normally tolerant person, not tyrannical about family funds. He had, however, recently asked the family to economize until their situation improved. It seemed probable that this woman felt some guilt over her purchase, not connecting her tension during the evening in the company of her husband with the purchase she made earlier. I suggested the connection and asked her to tell me what she probably had said to herself during the evening.

"Frankly, doctor, I didn't think of that dress at all. But maybe I was afraid to bring up the matter to Jim."

"Why?"

"He wouldn't have liked it, although he would have been nice about it outwardly."

"Then maybe you told yourself, 'Jim will be angry and dislike me for doing this.' "

"I doubt it. As I said, Jim often doesn't like what I do but seldom holds a personal grudge against me for doing it."

"Well, what else could you have been thinking?"

"I just don't know," she replied after thinking a few moments.

"Do you suppose you disliked yourself? Maybe you said something like: 'Now why did I go and do that? We really need our money for other things, and here I went and bought something I could have gotten later. That was really awfully selfish of me to burden the family further just because of my own childish impulses.'"

"Yes, that seems to ring a bell. I often blame myself for not thinking before I leap. That's one of my pitfalls: impulsive behavior. Now that I think of it, I'm sure you are right. I didn't want to admit to Jim that I couldn't control myself when he does it so beautifully all the time."

"And then what did you tell yourself?" I prodded, still trying to get her to see how she was being irrational.

"I didn't say anything beyond that, I don't think. I felt badly for what I had done. That's all."

"That can't be all of it, since we still don't know *why* you felt badly. What did you think of that made you blame yourself?"

"Oh, that's simple. I probably said I was bad for being so selfish."

"Right, now you've hit it on the nose. In other words, you believed you were a worthless person for doing a bad thing and that you should be blamed for it. Is that it?"

"Yes, I'm sure it is."

This conversation is only meant to demonstrate how the irrational ideas can be identified with the help of the counselor when it appears that the client is unable as yet to accomplish this. In Mrs. Stockton's case, she was suffering guilt and mild depression because she was judging her own worthwhileness by her behavior. It was Irrational Idea No. 3—"the idea that certain people are bad, wicked, or villainous, and that they should be severely blamed and punished for their villainy"—which was causing the emotional tension. Now that it was identified, we were ready for the next step.

2. *Challenging the Irrational Idea*

As long as Mrs. Stockton truly believed that she and her behavior were identical she would know no peace. Each time she performed less than ideally she would have to castigate herself neurotically. This she had been doing for years with no improvement in her behavior. Let us resume our session with her.

"All right, Mrs. Stockton, now that we know what you were thinking just before you got tense, let's look at those sentences and see if they make sense. Is it true that you are an awful person for being careless with money and that you ought to blame yourself?"

"Why, of course it is. I have no right to do such childishly selfish things when others are trying to make sacrifices. It's my fault, so whom should I blame except myself?"

"Why blame anyone?" I asked. "I agree with you that you've done a selfish and foolish thing, and that you are responsible for this act. But why does that mean you must hate yourself? Can't you accept the responsibility for this act and respect and accept yourself at the same time?"

"When I behave like that? How can I?"

"By believing and seeing that you are still as fine and worthwhile a human being after such an act as before. Right now you're telling yourself that you must never do wrong or you will become evil. The only way you'll ever live up to that impossible standard is to be a perfect saint. Frankly, I don't see wings sprouting from your shoulders.

So why shouldn't you commit perfectly human follies from time to time?"

"Now I don't want you to excuse me for my terrible actions," she protested. "I've done something serious and I shouldn't be forgiven for it too lightly."

"You prefer to suffer awhile and *then* be forgiven?"

"Yes, I think I have it coming," she said flatly.

"And just what do you think your self-inflicted suffering is going to do for you?"

"Maybe it'll help me grow up and stop this kind of irresponsible behavior."

"I'll buy that, *if* it'll help. Now tell me, haven't you been doing this thing for years, and haven't you been crucifying yourself afterward for years also? And isn't it true that this careless, selfish habit has been getting worse rather than better?"

"Yes, it has been. That's why I came to you for help. I'm getting so I can't stand myself. I even find myself being petty and self-centered where the children are concerned."

"Then isn't it high time you concluded that blaming yourself is *not* the way to stop this wrongdoing? How much proof do you need before you see that self-hatred gives you less and less confidence that you'll ever be able to change?"

She was silent momentarily but finally offered, "I had begun to wonder if I was hopeless."

"And why shouldn't you? People who hate themselves, call themselves awful names, and think they're the worst human beings alive, are bound to think they're beyond hope. Keep feeding yourself that kind of mental trash and you'll wind up fully believing it."

"But it's true. How can I possibly think otherwise?"

"By challenging your basic philosophy that *you* are a bad person merely because your *behavior* is bad. That's a false, untrue statement, and because you believe it you're upset. Show yourself that it's not true and it doesn't make sense. You'll feel better and *then* may be able to act better. Get your neurotic feelings out of the way first and you'll be able to do something about your problem."

"You want me to believe I'm just as good as my husband or other mature people when they control their desires and I don't? I really don't see why I don't deserve to be blamed."

"Look at it this way, Mrs. Stockton. The only way you could possibly never make a mistake is to be superhuman. If you were superhuman, it would make good sense to say you *could* go through life never goofing up. But we've already agreed you are not an angel. You are a fallible mortal as we all are. Furthermore, do you think you're the only one who behaves badly sometimes? Why do you dislike, even hate, yourself for doing something you would not hate others for?"

She laughed for the first time. "You think I've been too hard on myself by insisting I must be perfect at all times, is that it?"

"Sure it is. Relax the next time you commit an error. Tell yourself you're a fine person anyway, and that you need not blame yourself, but that you do not plan to ignore your wrongdoing. Instead, you will want to think over why the error was made and how you plan to avoid it in the future. You can only be that objective, however, if you keep yourself calm and undisturbed by not expecting godlike perfectionism from yourself."

Mrs. Stockton began for the first time to question the basic assumptions she had always lived by. This, in and of itself, will not modify her behavior. It is only a second step but an immensely important one. She will still need the counselor's assistance a number of times to help her overcome her self-blaming tendencies that are rooted in Irrational Idea No. 3.

3. *Practicing New Habit Patterns*

The irrational idea has been found. The client has been shown that it is irrational. Now this knowledge must find practical application in everyday life. In the past she had been hesitant to make purchases unless she first had her husband's approval. When she became tired of this passive, childlike dependency relationship, she would rebel with a splurge of independent buying, followed by the usual neurotic remorse, followed by an even greater dependency on him to take charge. In this way she gained at least some control over her habit, though this method was highly inefficient and emotionally very costly. She wondered how to proceed.

"I'll certainly try to think through what you've told me. It makes a lot of sense. I can begin to see how I've been treating myself very badly. I suppose in the future I'll have to change my thinking and perhaps avoid most purchases. Do you think I should turn the whole budget over to my husband and let him handle all the money?"

"What do you expect to gain by doing that?"

"I won't be reckless with money anymore, that's for sure."

"True, you'll never make a mistake if you don't try. But how will that solution help you learn to spend money more sensibly?"

"You mean that unless I try again I'll never really master

my problem? I'd be avoiding it if I turned it over to Jim, wouldn't I?"

"Yes, you'd be dumping it right into his lap. No, I'm afraid that's no answer. You must do exactly the opposite. Do all the necessary buying the two of you would normally do. But, while you're doing it don't tell yourself what a heel you'll be if you slip in an expensive item just for yourself. Consider it a normal slip and try again. Keep challenging your statement that you *need* this or that when really you mean you *want* this or that. Every time you think of a purchase go over this question in your mind. Sooner or later if you keep up the shopping *and the challenging,* you're going to be able to refuse items you once thought were indispensable. The only way you can learn to control that urge, however, is by exposing yourself to it over and over again and all the time trying to fight it with your new thinking. In time you'll have some success, and then you'll gain more confidence, which will lead to still more success. You're going to fail at times. You'll soon improve, however, if you don't blame yourself, but just say: 'Well, there I go again, convincing myself I needed these shoes merely because I liked them. What rubbish! I'd better think my next purchase over more carefully as I did last week. I did a fine job that time.' For homework I want you to go to the dress shop in your town at least once, look over what they have, keep telling yourself they're nice but not necessary, and walk out without buying a thing. Report back to me next week and we'll see what sort of progress you've made."

This is where new learning enters the picture. As long as we two are merely talking about changing behavior, all is safe and comfortable. Not until she is seriously tempted and then practices our new thinking has she really made any gains. Rational-emotive therapy insists upon the client's experiencing new behaviors and learning by trial and error. With her self-blaming tendencies now under examination, she can risk a mistake by shopping for a dress and possibly even buying it. However, being less nervous and confused, she may quite likely act responsibly.

In essence this is RET. Each case is different, yet still the same. Some clients will find it easier to locate the disturbing ideas than to challenge them. Others will need a great deal of help in discovering the irrational ideas but will show remarkable adeptness at seeing their irrationality once the ideas have been pointed out for them. Some will challenge these ideas convincingly during the first hour, others may require months. Some can change old habits with fewer than a half dozen visits, others barely after a year. Happily, practitioners of RET are able to report many instances of the former.

Dealing with Relapses

All habits once learned carry a momentum that can only be halted with active practice of another habit over a period of time. Time is the factor not sufficiently recognized as a special ingredient to change. However, many clients who are able to master new thinking skills and adopt new philosophies find later that the old habit, which was considered to have been mastered, has suddenly made a surprising reappearance.

A young mother whom I once counseled about her stubborn and defiant five-year-old son was quite proud of her progress in getting the lad to behave better. Being satisfied that she had truly learned better discipline methods, she decided to terminate therapy. As I often do before termination, I advised this mother as follows:

"I want to prepare you for occasional setbacks that you'll probably have with your son, Michael. Right now he's acting like an angel and all that undesirable conduct you complained of months ago has disappeared for some weeks now. Don't be too surprised, though, if the tantrums and stealing come back from time to time."

"But I thought he was over them. If he's going to do them again, should we be terminating now?" said the perplexed mother.

"It wouldn't matter when we terminated. We'd still have to face the likelihood that some of his patterns of behavior would almost spontaneously spring back to life."

"Would that mean I was slipping up on my job as a disciplinarian?"

"It might, but it could also have nothing to do with you at all. Old habits don't always die a rapid death. Some have a way of coming back to life when you least expect them. I remember once working with a man who was afraid he'd crash into the river if he drove over a bridge. I finally got him over that fear to the point where he was doing it all the time without a second thought. Then one day he called asking to see me because he had come to a bridge that morning and suddenly he couldn't cross it. Here was the old symptom again, apparently strong as ever, and it scared him considerably. Unfortunately, I had neglected to warn him before we terminated that such a thing might just happen, but that he needn't be upset over it."

"I'll bet he thought he'd have to start from scratch and fight the symptom again as he did the first time."

"Yes, that's exactly what he thought. It took fully an

hour before I got him calmed down enough to get him to see that the return of the symptom was not serious. It did not mean that he had made no gains at all, or that he would have to begin therapy from scratch. All it meant was that he hadn't been on his guard in approaching the bridge. He had alarmed himself as he had done earlier. If he could remain calm and decide to put into practice all he had learned, the next bridge would hardly scare him."

"You're telling me, then, that I can expect Michael to be his old devilish self again, but that I needn't be alarmed by that. And if I proceed to reapply my new discipline techniques, he'll snap back to where he is right now in a fraction of the time it's taken so far?"

"Correct. The setback may last no more than one incident or a day. Sometimes it lasts longer. In any event, correcting it a second time requires far less effort than it required at first. One more thing to be aware of: don't blame yourself and call yourself a failure when you see one of these spontaneous setbacks. They often happen despite one's best efforts. It would be a wonderful world if we learned everything perfectly the first time around, but we don't."

Sometimes the guilt and despair can be so deep after the return of a supposedly mastered symptom that the client begins to catastrophize wildly, placing himself in an anxiety cycle as he alarms himself over the sudden reappearance of the symptom. He becomes aware of the fact that he is alarmed and becomes doubly tense over *that*. Finally, he becomes even more frightened over the newly developed tension, and so on until he is in a near panic.

This can often be avoided if the spontaneous phenomenon is predicted for a client and explained in some detail. Here, knowledge is indeed a great soothing agent. The counselor who neglects to make his clients aware of it makes a great deal of unnecessary work for himself.

Another form of relapse, even more common than the one occurring after termination, is the one that takes place shortly after counseling begins. Quite often, after the first few interviews, the client makes rapid strides toward a calmer life. He is delighted with the progress he makes and is even surprised by it.

Such rapid strides are possible usually because he is very eager for some relief, because he has great faith in the counselor, and because his hopes are high. Such a mental attitude, if constantly maintained, would do wonders. Most clients come off this pinnacle of progress after a few sessions when pure faith can no longer sustain them, when hope must be nourished with results, and when hard-earned objectives must continually be worked on to be maintained. A plateau of reality will have been reached when the client realizes that the counselor is not a magician, his technique will work only when applied diligently, and that the client's emotional welfare is, in the final analysis, his own responsibility, not the doctor's, not even the medicine's. This disappointment *is* the relapse. If it is intense, the client may terminate. If mild, he will use it as a valuable insight into understanding the role *he* plays in the shaping of his life. He may then come to the realization that he alone has ultimate control over his feelings, that learning this control will demand a great deal of work from him no matter how many others also help him, and that *nothing else* short of this is going to work.

4
Teaching Self-acceptance

THE AVERAGE MINISTER WILL, IN THE COURSE OF HIS MINISTRY, encounter a great many clients suffering from anger and fear in all forms and degrees. Not the least of the problems he will deal with, however, are guilt and depression—the hallmarks of self-hate. If he learns to help his flock over these neurotic problems and no others, the pastor will have made an enormous contribution to its welfare.

How unfortunate that this necessary lesson is one of the most difficult to teach and, for some ministers, one of the most taxing to learn. Teaching self-acceptance will require a new outlook on old issues over which the minister is sure to be uncomfortable. Though this outlook will not be totally contrary to his theological position, it will most certainly go against his natural inclinations and those of his society. His present view of guilt and atonement will have to be totally reformulated, as will his thoughts about the immoral ideas that plague so many depressives.

Can such a sweeping change be adopted without doing violence to Christian doctrine? We believe so.

Biblical Justification for Self-love and Self-acceptance

A belated realization has come over the clerical community that an unappreciated assumption was included in the statement, "Thou shalt love thy neighbor as thyself" (Rom. 13:9b). Scripture takes it for granted that one should love oneself and *then* advises us to do likewise toward others. For some unknown reason the emphasis has always been placed on the neighbor rather than the self. Yet we cannot offer love to others if we have none to give, any more than we can offer physical strength if we are weak. To love others unselfishly we must have an *unconditional* regard for ourselves.

What is often thought of as love for others is a demand for acceptance because self-acceptance is lacking. The man who is trying to retain his wife's love on the excuse that he adores her has no regard for himself and uses her affections as a commodity. If she supplies it, he feels full of self-esteem and will love in return. If she denies it, he feels worthless and becomes unloving toward her. True love is possible only when his acceptance of himself will sustain him whether or not she returns his affections. This is the kind of self-regard this quotation from Romans is referring to. Yet so one-sided has been the interpretation of the Biblical lesson on love that this most vital human goal of self-love has been largely underplayed for centuries.

We shall soon see in the following remarks the serious consequences resulting from this myopia. For without self-acceptance we have self-hate. In place of joy over the sheer privilege of being alive, we have misery over the burden of getting through the day. In place of peace of mind, we have depression.[13]

Self-loathing keeps strange company, the ugliest of these brutes being guilt. Like a ringleader, it stirs up the passions of the internal mob until self-regard is trampled into the mud.

Is this truly the destiny of the errant as envisioned by religion? Does the Bible really ask that we torment ourselves over our misdeeds? Again, Rom. 3:23 denies any such understanding: "For all have sinned, and come short of the glory of God." No man is God. No man can hope, perhaps even for so long as a day, to be without sin. To expect better than this is to believe in God's perfectionistic control. Even if we were made in his image we must not believe that we were granted his nature. This simply means that sin is part and parcel of the human state and is forever inescapable. However, if such is the nature we were endowed with, why should we feel badly and guilty for behaving according to its limitations? Are we to be blamed for our imperfections and shortcomings? If so, then we are to be blamed for our sex, our height, and the color of our skin. Surely this is a preposterous notion. In deference to logical consistency we have no alternative but to agree that feeling guilty over our shortcomings is equally preposterous. If we cannot be gods, we must be men and accept the attribute of fallibility, which is the distinguishing feature between man and God.

An enlightened view of Scripture leaves no choice but to discredit guilt feelings completely. Religion cannot be a solace in times of trauma and also support the notion of guilt or self-blame. Spiritual tranquillity and guilt are anathema to each other.

As further support for this interpretation of Scripture, let us examine what is meant by Paul's remark in Phil. 3:13: "Brethren, I count not myself to have apprehended: but this one thing I do, forgetting those things which are behind, and reaching forth unto those things which are before . . ." Does he ask us to belabor our past deeds, to dwell on our errors, to punish ourselves with guilt? Or is this a plea to learn from our past so as to better the future? Is he not accepting all human behavior as being forgettable, not worthy of morbid attention? Rather, we should try to improve ourselves and look upon our misdeeds as stepping-stones to a richer life, not as weights to crush us. Here is a guilt-free philosophy worthy of imitation.

Theories of Depression and Guilt

The most widely held theory of depression is the psychoanalytic, which describes this pathological process in somewhat the following manner:[14] rather than vent hostility toward a loved object (because to do so would create intense guilt), the hating person deflects the flow of hostility from the object of his hatred back onto himself. In that way he hides his true feelings and guards against the loss of affection that he is sure would result from the overt expression of his feelings. At the same time he punishes himself for contemplating such a wicked act. In short, depression is a state of anger with oneself. If this self-directed anger is intense, the victim can experience depression of psychotic proportions. In most cases the self-hatred is mild and seen only as a neurotic depression, one which does not always require hospitalization. Such clients are often able to manage daily living, although they do so with great effort.

The most intense form of self-hatred is suicide. It too has a double function according to the analysts. The sufferer feels so totally unworthy and wicked that only the severest form of suffering can expiate his guilt by way of his death, and he can gain an indirect vengeance upon his frustrator. Needless to say, this often works in exactly that way.

The analytic view has merit as far as it goes. It tends to suggest, however, that all depressions are nothing more than deflected hostility turned inward. Not only is the notion of deflected hostility an incomplete one, but this theory fails completely to question the premise that guilt *must* result from hating a loved object. In other words, it assumes guilt to be a natural, unavoidable consequence of this instance. To say the least, this is debatable.

Gutheil [15] makes the questionable distinction between two types of depressions: the normal, physiologic reaction brought on by realistic frustrations such as loss of job, failure to win affection, etc., and neurotic depression, which arises in the absence of such experiences. But he fails to show us in what way the causes of "normal" depression differ from neurotic depression. We are left to assume that a depression is normal if it lifts when the frustration ends, but neurotic if the depression continues beyond the cessation of the frustration. Accordingly, the diagnosis cannot be made until it is known what happens to the difficult life situation. This is backward reasoning and not to be condoned.

How much more sensible it is to conclude that *all* depressions are neurotic regardless of their cause, for they create unnecessary pain to the self. Furthermore, it is difficult to understand why all neurotic depressions that result from difficult life situations must always involve a hostility turned back upon the self. Is it not possible for a person to be fired from a job, to become depressed, and to believe firmly that he deserves both? Yet if he is not deflecting hostility from his employer onto himself, then we must question the sweeping position of the analysts.

The notion of constitutional predisposition as espoused by Kraines and Campbell [16] holds some validity only to the extent that *all* irrational thinking is biologically predisposed. Faulty thinking, whether it creates anger, fear, or guilt, is so universal and appears so early in life that it leaves us no other conclusion. However, if by constitutional predisposition these investigators mean an unmodified human element, we must then take exception. Depression, along with all other neurotic reactions, can be unlearned, and—for all intents and purposes—will remain uninfluential for a lifetime once the proper thinking is adopted.

Incidentally, an important distinction must here be made between depression (which is regarded as a neurotic state) and sadness (which is considered quite normal).

One can hardly be gleeful over an untoward event. Such a reaction too would indicate disturbance. But one can be sensibly saddened by a death or loss of employment without also becoming completely nonfunctional. The difference depends almost entirely on how the event is perceived. Far too frequently a client will unconsciously utter to himself such statements as: "This is a *tragedy*. What a *catastrophe!* I'll *never* live through this."

The most casual observation will easily assure the neutral onlooker that this is simply not the truth. But the victim has used these expressions; he acts upon his perceptions; and then he acts appropriately in view of this labeling. If he is more critical in his initial appraisal of the situation, he may well concede that an event of some moment has transpired—an event which will call upon his powers of adjustment and leave him temporarily and moderately out of sorts. To this he can respond with a sense of somberness, tenseness, or annoyance, depending on conditions. He need never succumb to the more painful negative emotions of depression, anxiety, or hate. As counselors we are primarily concerned with the extremes of the emotional continuum, not the middle range. However, it happens that, upon taking a less histrionic view of things, the client is capable of narrowing his responsiveness to many of the milder forms of disturbance.

The Rational-Emotive Theory of Depression and Guilt

Depression has one or more of three sources: self-blame, self-pity, and other-pity. Anyone practicing these neurotic thought habits will inevitably become moody, saddened, morose—in short, depressed. These thought patterns always introduce that emotion. Specifically, the irrational thoughts involved are one or more of the following six: Irrational Idea No. 1: "The idea that it is a dire necessity for an adult human being to be loved or approved by virtually every significant other person in his community." Not feeling loved by others, the neurotic concludes that *he* is not worthwhile. This act is synonymous with self-blame. Irrational Idea No. 2: "The idea that one should be thoroughly competent, adequate, and achieving in all possible respects if one is to consider oneself worthwhile." Failing to attain the saintly purity and godlike perfection we all strive for, the neurotic hates himself relentlessly. This is one of the more common causes for self-blame. Irrational Idea No. 3: "The idea that certain people are bad, wicked, or villainous and that they should be severely blamed and punished for their villainy." Even though this idea usually creates hostility toward others, it is just as effective in creating anger at the self when the *self* performs imperfectly. Other-blamers can just as easily turn tables on themselves and become self-blamers. Irrational Idea No. 4: "The idea that it is awful and catastrophic when things are not the way one would very much like them to be." This is the idea that leads to self-pity as well as anger. Irrational Idea No. 5: "The idea that human unhappiness is externally caused and that people have little or no ability to control their sorrows and disturbances." "Normal" reactive depressions supposedly result from precisely those causes alluded to by this false notion. Loss of employment, loss of love, lack of achievement, etc., are all regarded as unquestioned criteria for depression. And lastly, Irrational Idea No. 10: "The idea that one should become quite upset over other people's problems and disturbances." This, along with Idea No. 5 (unhappiness is externally caused), accounts for depression of the third type: excessive empathy or other-pity. A parent can easily become depressed if he knows his child is friendless and rejected at school.

It can readily be seen that depression is a common reaction to different problems. Certainly it is more complex than the mere inward turning of hostility. Though this is sometimes true and well described under the idea that people are bad and should be punished, it hardly accounts for the many faces of depression. Any experienced counselor sees more depressions related to the idea that people must be perfect in order to feel worthwhile than to any other single cause. In this instance, there is practically never any hostility directed at another person. The hatred is almost always directed at the self as soon as the imperfect behavior is realized.

Does Guilt Have Value?

The notion is widely prevalent that guilt has a great value in deterring people from gross wrongdoings, and the greater the sin, the more intense the feeling of guilt must be to control the act in the future.[17] This is both supported and refuted by closer examination. It is doubtless true that many acts of misconduct are averted because the culprit would feel intensely miserable if he committed the act. Yet, it is equally true that many sinners keep repeating their sins, doing so in ever greater degree as they experience the keenest pangs of a guilty conscience. How can we reconcile these contradictory findings? Simply by realizing honestly that guilt is inefficient in controlling behavior. Anything that works only occasionally, or that costs as much in suffering as depression does, must be questioned. In other words, when guilt does work, is it worth the pain it creates?

Let us see what often happens. A man assumes vocational responsibilities that he cannot handle and begins to do failing work. His guilt is considerable. In time he cannot sleep. Soon he loses his appetite and then asks to be excused from his duties. His wife begins to worry about him and becomes upset also. Expensive drugs somehow fail to tranquilize him. As income in the family decreases, the man feels guilty over the hardships he is placing on his family. His minister is summoned to help him. Perhaps this too fails to lessen the mighty force of self-blame within this victim. Then his parents become alarmed, adding their worry to his. They lose sleep and appetite out of concern for their son. Perhaps they feel it necessary to fly to his side, thereby using their meager resources. If the client's depression continues, he will finally be sent to an institution for drug or shock treatment—another strain on the family. If the hospital successfully returns him to his home within weeks or months, and if he dares trust himself at his job again, he may still be eternally haunted by the memory of the episode.

Is this farfetched, unreasonable, improbable? No! Such a progression of events is commonly seen in the field of counseling. How does one evaluate the work of guilt in this case? Is the man less likely to fail again? Hardly. He did not want to do poorly the first time. Now, in a distraught state, he is *more* likely to be on edge, nervous, uncertain, and thereby more vulnerable to another depression than before. One could not devise a more inefficient method to avoid a future mishap.

The protest may arise that we would not want this victim to suffer so over an uncontrollable event. "Guilt should operate only when the evil deed could have been avoided, when it was committed out of selfishness, greed, revenge, or other controllable cause," you insist. There are three arguments against this assertion:

1. People who react with guilt in the first place seem to find it very difficult to distinguish between circumstances when an event is accidental (and no fault of theirs) and when an event is deliberate (for which they may be held responsible). A woman, for example, once related feeling very guilty one evening while out for a walk. A car drove up and the driver propositioned her. She had done noth-

ing whatever to encourage this advance, yet she felt keenly guilty over having been selected by him as his target. As she was a confirmed self-blamer, she had long learned to attribute any mishap to herself.

2. An event is not under control when motivated by neurotic emotions (irrational thinking). A father who brutally batters his child cannot control himself at the moment he is at the height of his fury. He is, at that moment, subject to the training he was exposed to all his life. People are taught by their parents, friends, and teachers that one cannot help becoming very angry when exposed to constant frustration. This father may have been listening to his child cry far into the night, not allowing him much-needed sleep. Sometime during those fitful hours he probably told himself: "I can't stand this another minute. That kid is driving me nuts. I'll teach him to keep me awake. He'll really get something to cry about."

These are the thoughts he regards as perfectly normal. He does not know he is arousing himself emotionally. Once angered, he cannot judge or care about the damage he is doing. Once set into motion by his irrationality, he is as much a victim of his thoughts as the child is of the father's behavior. In my opinion he is in the same circumstances as the man who tried to work beyond his abilities. He too need feel no guilt. Literally speaking, they have both been victims of forces outside themselves: their neurotic training.

This viewpoint will doubtless arouse disagreement. People will say in dismay: "Once again the psychologists are telling us, as they always have, that no one is responsible for what he does. It's always someone or something else that's at fault."

This is *not* our present viewpoint. To understand the

difference we must distinguish between two responsibilities, not one.

It is not sensible or right to say that we humans are responsible for misdeeds, stupidities, or emotionalisms we were taught and trained to practice. If I have been trained to get my way by acting hurt, peevish, and finally angry, that is the responsibility of my parents, just as the language I speak is credited to them. *Overcoming* the problem, however, is *my* responsibility. No one can change me but myself. This may seem monstrously unfair, yet this is how it is. *We* must be rational about situations if we are to control them. To return to our example of the child-beating father: he is not responsible for *having* poor control over his frustrations initially, but he is responsible for correcting that weakness. One of my clients resentfully asked me once: "Why should I be the one to go through all the work and sweat to straighten out the mess my parents made? They are responsible for the way I was raised. Why don't they do something about my problem?"

"Because they can't, not any longer," I answered. "If you were still a youngster, I'd do just that. I'd instruct them on how to undo the lazy and irresponsible habits they taught you. Now you're an adult. Like it or not, the problem is yours. It would be the same if someone hurt you physically. You might be entirely innocent of the injury. However, if you wanted to get over the pain, you're the one who would have to make the trips to the doctor's office. You'd have to take your medicine every four hours. And if the other party was very poor, you'd even have to pay for your treatment. Of course, you could neurotically tell yourself you're not going to take care of the injury because you didn't cause it. In that case you might die. That's your choice too, I suppose."

3. Guilt, if it is intense, strangles the energy needed to correct the deed. This is the third argument against believing that one should feel guilty over misdeeds which are controllable (not accidental). What has happened has happened, and all the regrets in the world will not turn back the clock. Once the damage is done we can only hope to profit from the costly lesson rather than use it as a cudgel against ourselves. To profit from it we must *calmly* think about the misdeed and how it could be avoided in the future. A guilty person is not thinking preventively, only self-accusingly.

A distinction should here be made between *being* guilty and *feeling* guilty. The former refers to responsibility, to the person or thing that caused an event. A man who sleeps with a woman other than his wife is guilty of adultery, that is, he, not someone else, is responsible for a sin. That is not the same as saying, however, that he should *feel* guilty because he *is* guilty, for then we are asking him to admit to not one, but two conditions: (*a*) that he has misbehaved, and (*b*) that he is a worthless human being for having misbehaved. We contend on psychological and theological grounds that this is not helpful or even valid. If the man will accept the fact of being guilty, he has every hope of modifying that behavior in the future. If he thinks he should feel guilty as well, then he may punitively drive himself to commit other misdeeds.

Intrinsic and Extrinsic Values

We have seen how guilt and depression are caused by harsh internalized thoughts aimed at self-blame. This recalls Irrational Idea No. 3—"the idea that certain people are bad, wicked, or villainous and that they should be severely blamed and punished for their villainy." This idea is usually an outcome of another thought, Irrational Idea No. 2—"the idea that one should be thoroughly competent, adequate, and achieving in all possible respects if one is to consider oneself worthwhile." These perfectionistic thoughts arise after an act has been committed in the light of which the person judges himself. For him, his value lies in the value of his acts. This brings up the matter of intrinsic and extrinsic values.

If I play bridge well, I am certain to have value to others who also play bridge. My extrinsic value (my value to others) would then be high, and I would be quite correct and rational in making this appraisal. However, I might also conclude that my value to myself had also risen because others thought so well of me. I would then believe my intrinsic value had increased along with my extrinsic value. That is, I would think I had become more valuable and worthwhile to myself, *because* others had said I was important and valuable to them.

By the same token, it is concluded by those confused over intrinsic and extrinsic values that a person's worth as a human diminishes as he or she loses value to others. As an example, if I do not lecture well, but most of my acquaintances do, I might conclude incorrectly that my intrinsic value was low because my importance to my friends, as a lecturer, was also low.

People in all walks of life and of all ages make this error repeatedly. The salesman with the lowest sales record for the month concludes he is not only a poor salesman (extrinsic value) but a pitiful human being as well (intrinsic value). The adolescent girl who does not make the ranks of the cheerleaders concludes she is not as desirable as they, *and* that she, therefore, is undesirable to herself.

The mother who is doing a thoroughly bad job of mothering not only judges her skill in maternal matters as being deficient (an ostensibly true observation) but she believes *she* is as worthless a *person* as she is a mother. In each of these examples we see the person passing judgment on himself on the basis of skills he has or has not mastered. These skills can be of any type: physical, mental, social or ethical. Yes, these skills can be ethical, for moral behavior is learned no differently than are football, arithmetic, dancing, or cooking. Instruction, followed by practice, followed by evaluation and correction, repeated as often as necessary—these are the steps that master all skills.

Inability to perform a skill up to expectation should never be the basis for determining one's worth as a person. The whole process is so riddled with logical contradictions that one can only marvel that it is practiced so universally. To begin with, if our talents, achievements, or skills really reflect what we are to ourselves, then how is a man to respond to opposite behaviors? Is he worthless because he drinks too much but wonderful because he is an outstanding teacher? Clearly, he cannot be worthless *and* worthwhile at one and the same time—not to himself, that is. Such statements make sense only when referring to the separate behaviors, for it is reasonable to suppose that his drinking holds no value for his family, while his teaching does have value to his students.

Furthermore, must he despise himself because he is deficient in one skill (sobriety) while being perfectly capable in many others (driving, public speaking, checkers, etc.)? No one is all-capable. Even the outstanding among us has his superiors. To equate personal worth with demonstrable skill is to make every living soul *personally* worthless, for who is without fault and who is without sin?

Finally, how meaningful can a concept be if it has no stability? Is a mother worthless because she is inadequate at raising her first son, worthwhile if she does better with her middle son, and worthless again if she is stumped over the third? And when she deals with all three at once—what value does this mean she should have for herself? We become lost in a maze of unanswerable questions. Extrication is possible only through the separation of the two concepts: behavior and self. This is the only means of self-acceptance as well. To think well of one's self even though one's behavior is unsatisfactory is the key to high personal regard. Many have self-esteem, but it is based on good works, not intrinsic value. Should their customary exemplary behavior falter ever so slightly, their personal regard diminishes. Such is not the way to mental health. Depression of the self-blame variety is created not by disapproving of one's faulty behavior, but by believing that one's own value has diminished because the behavior was faulty and that one *is* as one behaves.

What leads us to believe that we have intrinsic value? Do we offer the concept because it is a pleasant one, or does there appear to be a rational basis for it?

On earth, at least, it would seem correct to believe that man's greatest blessing is life. His existence is his personal treasure. Without it he is nothing. Life, however, is inseparable from the body that contains it. A human form without life has no purpose, seeks no goals, derives no pleasures, has no expectations, and has no intelligence or skills with which to fulfill its potential. A human form with life always has some degree of intelligence, has the potential to develop some skill, can set goals to satisfy its potential, however low they may be. Accepting this state of affairs, that form, or body, can derive pleasure from its life. Regardless of what others feel for that living form, the fact that the physical body has life means it has a destiny all its own, quite apart from the prejudices of other bodies with life. It says in effect: "I have the capacity to make the most of the life in me—to make my body be as productive and as pleased as my talents allow—and this is true regardless of how much more talent or intelligence other bodies have to be productive or to enjoy life, and whether or not I use my talents. My body has value, therefore, because it has life. What I *do* may be judged by others or by myself. But my existence, which makes that doing possible, can never lose in value to my body. The flesh has value only as it has life. If it has life, it has worth."

The depressive disagrees with this position. When his behavior is faulty he feels disgust with (*a*) his behavior, (*b*) the body that performed the misdeed, and (*c*) the *life* that made it possible for the body to sin. If his errors continue, the disgust will turn to hatred and he will then think of destroying that life by destroying the body. He fails to see that life in an imperfect organism is not at fault. The fault lies with the unreasonable expectation that imperfect and fallible forms should behave without error. Instead of merely correcting his faulty ways if possible, the self-blamer blames life itself. It is then that he feels death is preferable to life. In this matter we are impotent to demonstrate an untruth, for we have no evidence that life is better than death. We simply make the assumption which must frankly be accepted on faith: that life itself is a state preferable to death. Let those who disagree seek the juggernaut!

In counseling, the preceding philosophical distinction is often difficult to make. The use of examples helps. The young divorcee, guilty because she has turned over custody of her five children to her husband, is shown that she may be "bad" at numerous skills, such as opera singing, skeet shooting, shipbuilding, etc., but that she does not need to regard herself as being a bad person because of these failings. Why is it then logical to conclude that she is a bad person because she is a bad mother? Abandoning her children to her husband might well be regarded as a mistake but hardly proves that she is awful, wicked, or worthless for having made the error in the first place. She is never bad and worthless, regardless of what misdeed she commits, for all mistakes are committed for perfectly good reasons: stupidity, ignorance, or emotional disturbance. If she will learn how to be a better mother, her ignorance will vanish. When she learns to be less disturbed, her vengeful, impulsive, immature behavior will diminish. If she were mentally deficient (stupid), she ought certainly never to blame herself either, for she simply would lack the intelligence to know better.

If such debates do not suffice to relieve the self-blame, the counselor can go into another example. One that I have found to be helpful runs as follows:

"Mrs. Jones, I'd like to show you why you're wrong about hating yourself and believing you have no value to yourself. Suppose your eyes are not as good as mine. I wouldn't wish I had them, would I? Now, would you say that your eyes are no good to you just because I don't want them? Of course not. You certainly aren't going to pluck them out and throw them away. They're all the eyes you've got. Even if you can barely see with them, they still are immensely valuable to you though they aren't to me. Well, why do you go on believing you're no good for yourself just because your husband doesn't want you anymore? You're all you've got. You have life and the potential to enjoy it. Don't go hating your life because you displease someone else, any more than you'd blind yourself because others had no use for your eyes."

In place of the idea of eyes, one might use the terms "children" or "spouse" in the above illustration. Surely she would not desert *herself* merely because her training was found wanting or because she was not totally approved of by others?

The clergyman who fails to love his sinners even while deploring their sins had better not offer himself as a counselor. He can only increase his client's self-loathing and bring that person close to the brink of suicide.

The Thought and the Deed

The Bible says that "whosoever looketh on a woman to lust after her hath committed adultery with her already in his heart" (Matt. 5:28). This is a clear statement that expresses complete agreement between a deed contemplated and a deed fulfilled. Taken literally by millions, it is the indirect cause of an immense amount of guilt and anxiety. Therefore, how is the pastor to assist the victim of obsessive thoughts without violating his belief in the Scriptures? Can he be of service in relieving the neurotic distress while not denying his principles? Fortunately, yes. Such thoughts do not have to be whitewashed or denied as wrong in order to bring comfort to the client. We shall see after a brief diversion how this is possible in rational-emotive counseling.

Unwelcomed thoughts arise on two kinds of occasions:

by accident and after a frustration. A mother who used her scissors as a pointer, stuck them once into her child's cheek quite by chance as she was showing him where the cookies were. Not only was she filled with guilt but the thought soon occurred to her that she might be capable of the most awful cruelties to her boy. For several days she was not herself until she decided the thought was preposterous. She reasoned that she had nothing but love for her son, that her accident signified nothing but carelessness on her part, and that it could be avoided easily enough in the future.

A father almost killed his son by firing his hunting rifle at a rustle in the brush which he thought was made by an animal. He was momentarily stunned by the thought, "My God, I almost killed Johnny." So unnerved was he by his experience that he began to wonder if it was really accidental. For months afterward the painful thought, "Did I really want to murder my son?" plagued the man relentlessly.

Most unwelcomed thoughts, however, take possession of their victim slowly, after a period of frustration has occurred. A man, long discontent with his marriage, may gradually wonder more and more what an affair would do for him until the thought becomes so strong he fears leaving his home alone lest he give in to this temptation. A boy, long oppressed by a harsh mother, gradually and obsessively feared smothering her with a pillow while she slept.

Most of us have been subject to these surprising thoughts and fortunately have not taken them seriously. When such thoughts do take root, however, they seem, among other things, to be followed by two swift reactions: intense guilt feelings and a determination not to have such thoughts again. Ironically enough, these two reactions feed the momentum. The more intense the guilt, the greater the desire to control future distasteful thoughts. This leads to fear lest they not be controlled, thus usually leading to failure, which brings on more guilt. Not only are the original thoughts not controlled, but under the influence of this neurotic state new thoughts emerge. The thought, "Could I push my wife out of the window?" might now be accompanied by: "Could I throw myself out of the window?" Finally, the most damaging belief takes hold: "I must be losing my mind. I am hopeless. I should be locked up."

Self-blame over wicked thoughts is totally unreasonable. Once again: man is fallible. An evil idea is as natural a phenomenon as is the aging process. Fallible beings cannot be held blameworthy for doing what they are incapable of controlling. Secondly, self-blame does not reduce these thoughts. Self-acceptance does. It is not until he accepts himself despite these ideas that a man can regain enough composure to think rationally and eventually to reduce their incidence. Thirdly, it seems utterly unreasonable to blame oneself for not having controlled a thought when one does not know beforehand that such a thought exists, or when it will emerge again. The only time a person knows he is thinking wickedly is *after* he has the wicked idea. If he knew that during the next minute he would get the idea of killing someone, we might then expect him to do something about avoiding such a thought. Obviously this is impossible, for he cannot know a thing consciously until it emerges into his awareness.

The remedy for this pitiful state lies in observing three steps:

1. Attempt to teach the client self-acceptance and self-

forgiveness. Regardless of how evil the thought is, he must be shown that the thought is truly alien and separate from him, the result of past and faulty training, which he can overcome if he practices sensible thinking techniques. No attempt should be made to pretend that his thoughts are really benign and innocent, for the client will feel that his predicament is not fully appreciated. Instead, we agree that such thoughts are wrong and worth removing, but are not reflections of his worth. As we would not find fault with *him* for possessing low intelligence, poor memory, or faulty coordination, so we do not concern ourselves with his personal self. His unwelcomed thoughts arise as a result of natural propensities and continue to arise because of guilt and fear. We show him that increased self-blame will soon cause him to regard himself as an incorrigible sinner and will bring on more unacceptable thoughts. This is the first step toward self-control.

2. Show the client that as with unacceptable behavior, so also with unacceptable thoughts: the harder one tries to control them, the more uncontrolled they become. A person is not likely ever to feel free of torment if he constantly thinks: "Lord, I've got to stop having these thoughts of killing my wife. I mustn't think about that anymore. What kind of wretch am I, that I can even think of pushing her down the stairs? Great God! There I go again, devising other ways of killing her. When am I going to stop having such ideas?" Even while he is trying desperately not to entertain such notions, his time is spent *only* with them. To be free of this worry he must also be free of the worry of their control, for one leads to the other. For this reason we encourage him *not* to try so hard. He will be in greater control if he relaxes over these ideas, gets less panicky, and worries less over their possi-

ble return. Being calm and indifferent about their return almost always reduces their intensity.

3. Show the client how unlikely it is that his thoughts will take shape in action. The argument from point two above is usually questioned on the grounds that one cannot take an idea lightly if it is likely to result in a tragic action. Often such impulses have plagued the client for months or years. This fact is an excellent weapon for the counselor, since he can prove to the client the great improbability of these thoughts actually taking form in actions. One such client was reminded that he had had thoughts of killing his mother for well over twenty years. In that span of time the thought had probably occurred hundreds of times. If such a thought could actually lead to murder, why hadn't it done so before? Wasn't it more reasonable to conclude from this evidence that all that would happen the next time he thought of murdering his mother was exactly what had happened so many times in the past? The precise sequence of feelings and events was carefully studied and he was shown that (*a*) his mother did something very frustrating to him; (*b*) he had the hateful thought of wishing to see her dead; (*c*) he became nervous, depressed, and fearful that he might carry out his wish; and (*d*) after a day at the longest, this feeling passed and he recovered enough to live with her until the next episode. It was then emphasized that *that was all* that happened. The next time he faced this sequence of events he was almost certain to go through these *four* steps. He had never in hundreds of trials gone to the fifth step, which would have been the actual murder itself.

As he could see the reasonableness of this evidence he lost his fear of the final dreaded step and this permitted us to work on his guilt at simply having the thought.

Here is a task the average clergyman will not relish. In all probability the pastor will have to go through the same rigorous challenging of his own beliefs that the client must go through, before he can speak convincingly. This task will naturally be particularly difficult for those pastors who follow the Bible literally. However, it is not necessary to reject religious training to help victims of obsessive thinking. I have helped a number of such clients over this problem without at any time questioning their faith.

Psychological Atonement

There is a belief among the clergy that sins and wrongdoings must be accompanied by mental pain and suffering in order to make the sinner want to atone. Some of the clergy further believe that atonement through personal anguish and remorse is a sound exchange for the frustrations that others may have suffered at the sinner's hands. It is not sufficient, for example, to make reparations through the payment of damages for angrily destroying another's property. It is also expected that the guilty party should suffer emotionally for his careless deed in order to provide a guarantee that he has seen the error of his ways and will try to be more careful in the future. The fear seems to be that the sinner will not particularly care whether he controls himself again unless he goes through an emotional upheaval as well. Atonement, as thus viewed, demands a physical reparation (such as making good the damages, etc.) *and* an intense emotional reaction (such as guilt, depression, or remorse). Modern psychological findings cast serious doubt as to the wisdom of this prevalent belief.

The idea that one must suffer adverse consequences for one's harmful actions is eminently sound. Unless the wrongdoer suffers for his mistakes, there will be no basis to motivate him to change. All of us are amply aware of this simple principle in such daily matters as obeying traffic regulations, paying our taxes, etc. We obey these laws generally to avoid such consequences as fines or imprisonment. When we do break them, proper restitution is demanded of us, and if the penalties are harsh enough, we probably obey the law henceforth. This would not happen, of course, unless the consequences of our behavior hurt *more* than the satisfactions we obtained from them, and if we were not neurotically punishing ourselves.

We have been speaking of illegal behavior. What of immoral behavior? There is no law against a man cursing his wife until she cries. How can he be made to suffer unpleasant consequences from these acts unless he is taught to hate himself for being a tyrant? And why should he want to stop his bullying unless the behavior leads to a fair degree of personal distress for himself, supposedly through the method of guilt?

These are profound and valid questions which must be answered if the clergy is ever to adopt other views. Not one, but several reasons may be shown why this ancient view should be amended.

1. Guilt often generates more sin. This point has already been discussed but bears repetition. When an evil act has been committed, the person who blames himself for that act (that is, hates his action *and* himself) will focus on his own worthlessness rather than on how to correct the act in the future. His attention will have shifted from the problem to himself. In his mind he will mull over

such thoughts as: "What a heel I am. God almighty, how I've sinned. Lord, how terrible a person I must be. I can't stand myself."

This attitude does little good, either to the man or his victim. For example, if a man has hit someone with his car, it is futile for him to pay such exclusive attention to what an awful person he is. At that moment the victim has absolutely no interest in how sorry and remorseful the driver is or how awful he considers himself to be. We would want him to focus on the *deed,* not on himself. His thoughts ought to be: "Holy smokes, I've run over someone. He's lying in front of the car. I'd better call an ambulance and get him to the nearest hospital." This is sane thinking. The former is not.

The minister may well agree that at the moment a harmful or evil act is committed, it is better to focus on it instantly so as to avoid needless further harm. But after that has been taken care of, after the victim has been deposited in the hospital, shouldn't he then blame himself in the hope he will surely drive more carefully in the future? The answer is No, not if he gets behind the wheel with such thoughts as: "What's the matter with me? I never do anything right. I deserve to be horsewhipped for some of the dumb stunts I pull. I can't stand myself. I *must* watch out that nothing else happens."

These thoughts can only make a person so preoccupied and fearful of another incident that he can easily run over someone else. If he really wants to improve his driving, he must focus calmly on his faulty driving habits, not on his value as a human being. Before he drives off from the hospital, he should be studying his original mistake in somewhat the following manner:

"Let's see now. I bumped into that fellow as I was coming up to the corner. Funny I didn't see him. He must have been there and chances are I did see him but it didn't register for some reason. I wonder why? Did I do something when I neared the intersection? Now I remember! I was listening to the radio and I suddenly got static and couldn't hear the game score. It was while I was adjusting the radio that I bumped into him. It seems to me the thing I've learned from all this is to give driving my full attention when I near an intersection and not to touch anything else in the car unless I'm out on the open road. If I'm careful to keep this in mind, I probably won't have this kind of accident again."

This is what is meant by focusing on the problem. This kind of thinking, and it alone, is what is needed to correct inefficient or evil behavior. The individual could, of course, go through this critical analysis and *then* blame himself and bring on mental suffering. But what would he gain? It profits no one for him to suffer mentally. When he has attempted to learn by trial and error, he has done all that we can expect of him and *all that will do any good.*

"And what about the cold-blooded murderer or thief?" you ask. "Does he not act ruthlessly precisely because he has no guilt?" I confess that it seems logical to suppose that a strong dose of guilt would have prevented numerous child beatings, rapes, or thefts. This, however, is not totally true either. The psychopath who feels no remorse for his evil acts feels thus because he genuinely does not think that his acts are evil. The victim he robbed "had plenty of money." The girl he raped "teased him." The child he beat "learned a good lesson." *If* he is remorseful, it would tend to indicate that he is seeking self-punishment and is living up to his mental image of himself as an evil ne'er-do-well.

When we acquaint ourselves with the moral standards of many antisocial characters we soon learn that they do feel remorse for their misdeeds—as *they* define them. One adolescent may feel very ashamed because he did not participate actively enough in the beating of a robbery victim. Another may hate himself for performing an act of kindness for which his associates may label him "sissy." The guilt of such people is often connected with acts for which most of us would feel pride.

2. A second argument against the guilt-is-necessary school of thought is: atonement is already part of the corrective process. Seneca suggested that crime can never go unpunished because the punishment of the crime lies in the crime itself. This is not always true by any means, as we all know. Crime often pays. And if the criminal can rationalize "properly," he need not even suffer mental disturbance for it. Seneca's thought ought to be rephrased: crime can never go unpunished *if the wrongdoer wishes to change his ways,* since the punishment of crime lies in the crime itself. Here we have used uncritically the term "crime" to refer to a wide assortment of behavior such as sins, accidental wrongdoings, or simply neurotic habits.

Each time a kleptomaniac steals, that habit is strengthened. Each time a young man deliberately keeps to his own company because of his shyness, the tendency to isolate himself is strengthened and the symptom of shyness is increased. The same may be said for the alcoholic, the thief, the depressive, and so on.

This means that the process of correction becomes, through habit, much more difficult if and when the victim of these patterns decides that he wants to conquer them. With every repetition of the habit, the task of eliminating it becomes more difficult. In almost the same fashion, the task of losing weight is made more difficult with every calorie consumed.

Atonement becomes a built-in feature of these habits in that their correction simply cannot be accomplished without much hard work. He who has enjoyed the undisciplined and irresponsible life the longest suffers the most in making the change. It is hardly necessary to burden him further with what we might call "religious atonement," when he has this intrinsic "psychological atonement" to contend with. The more he understands how his refusal to change eventually makes change more difficult, the sooner he recognizes his responsibility in his own misery. Overcoming well-established habits, whether they be smoking or worrying, demands constant effort. Clients are often quite sorry that they allowed behavior problems to continue so long, and they know they are paying the price for their lassitude. This regret, this extra burden to change *is* atonement. It is implicit within the corrective process.

3. Thirdly, morality demands less immorality, not more suffering. Religion and psychology are interested in helping people behave according to the standards of each. Religion expects moral behavior, psychology expects rational behavior. Both tacitly hope there is much in common between them. Yet often, ironically, the end to which religion aspires (improved moral conduct) seems unsatisfactory to the clergy. The charge is made that an apparent change to ethical behavior is unconvincing and insufficient unless the individual is truly contrite for his misdeeds. There is something insincere, some clergymen insist, if a man changes his ways in a carefree manner. Yet, is there? If the behavior is really changed, what else can we ask for? Are we not all essentially interested in im-

proved behavior, so that human suffering may be reduced? How can we demand, then, that the sinner suffer while he is in the very act of change? Are we not being equally guilty of harm to the human race as is our client? The sinner is as much entitled to our kindness as is the victim. We disapprove of the sinner's thoughtless acts that bring pain to others. Have we any right to ask the sinner to suffer, simply to prove his contrition? In short, is there more action needed to prove contrition than to prove the desire to change?

It must be plainly seen that when we ask for a change to moral behavior and get it, we have done our best and should let the matter rest. To insist on suffering in addition to the suffering already necessary for change is almost revengeful. This means that we should be content with the success of helping an embezzler calmly decide that his stealing is wrong and that he will change his ways at once. The law will rightfully have unfinished business with him. The pastor and counselor, however, are finished with him when the objectionable behavior is controlled, whether it be done as lightheartedly as making a joke or after intense soul-searching. "For whom the LORD loveth he correcteth" (Prov. 3:12). Note the emphasis on correction and the absence of any mention of revenge.

Depression and Self-blame: Mrs. Botin

A female in her mid-forties was referred to me by her priest, who had had little success in helping her over the third depressive episode in ten years. Hospitalization was required for both previous bouts and it seemed that she would certainly have to return unless her mood changed. In addition to not eating or sleeping well, she was very irritated and impatient with her children, and this added to her already heavy emotional load.

I surmised from her history that she must have been blaming herself over a past misdeed and encouraged her to speak of it. Finally she said: "I've never told my husband that I had an illegitimate child before I married him. This bothered me even more. I've wanted to tell him a million times but I can't. I know things won't be the same after he knows. He'll despise me."

"And you believe it's what you did that is depressing you?"

"Of course. I committed a terrible sin by having a child out of wedlock and now I'm sinning more by deceiving my husband."

"I can see what you mean, Mrs. Botin. Tell me, why are you making yourself suffer over these sins?"

"I can't help myself, doctor. I can't forgive myself for being the way I am."

"In that case you're going to get more depressed and wind up in the state hospital again, I'm afraid."

The counselor refuses to pull any punches. He "levels" with her and leaves no doubt in her mind whose responsibility it will be if she is committed.

"I am? You can't help me?" she said, fighting the tears.

"I can help you all right, but only if you'll help yourself."

"I'll do anything, doctor. I just can't go back to the hospital again."

"Then stop hating yourself, Mrs. Botin. It's that simple."

"How can I do that when you know what I've committed?"

"That doesn't make any difference. It is not what you

did that's depressing you, it's what you think of yourself for having committed those sins. You think you're a worthless, evil person for having done a bad thing. You're judging your *self* by your *actions*. The only way you could ever avoid not becoming depressed under those circumstances is to behave perfectly."

"I don't want to be perfect. God knows I have many faults. But to do what I did . . . that's something no one should do."

"You mean no one should do things like that *if* they are perfect. You just said you weren't superhuman, so why hate yourself for committing perfectly normal sins? Mortal human beings *should, must,* commit sins. They can't escape them any more than they can escape death."

"I know people will sin. But did I have to become pregnant out of wedlock and bring a helpless child into the world?"

"Of course you didn't have to. But you did. That proves you were a stupid, love-struck, young woman who didn't know any better. You were too young to have good judgment. Do you suppose you would have gotten into that mess if you had been more mature and less passionate?"

"No, I suppose not. I certainly didn't let it happen again."

"That's my point. When your hard-learned experience sank through to you, your judgment matured and you did not allow yourself the freedom you did before your judgment was ripe. So it's a matter of being too naïve that caused you to take the wrong road. You corrected the naïveté and the problem was solved. What else could you do? Have you improved your living, for example, and behaved better because you hated yourself these many years?"

It almost always helps to describe self-harming techniques and how little is gained by being loyal to them.

"No, I guess not."

"No guessing about it. You got yourself so depressed that you were hospitalized twice. That was hard on your family, wasn't it, to say nothing of what it was on you?"

"You make it sound like I should completely forget about it and act like nothing happened."

"Not entirely. You could have simply told yourself: 'Now look here, Jane, you let your passions run away with you and an innocent child may have to suffer. I'm sorry for that but can see to it that the child is adopted by fine parents. Hereafter, however, I will simply have to avoid a sexual attachment until I'm married. This has been a real lesson to me. I don't like doing harmful things like that and if I watch out from now on, I can do better. In the meantime, I can go on liking myself. I'm not bad even though I did a bad thing. I committed a sin because I'm imperfect. No one can go on forever without doing *some* wrong.'"

"Now, Mrs. Botin, had you been thinking like that, you couldn't have been depressed in a million years. You would have profited by your sin without forgetting it. But you would not have used it to hurt yourself and your family as you so often have."

"I just can't get it through my head that I'm as good as others after what I've done, especially now, after the way I've been screaming at my children."

"Okay, let's take that as another example. Here you're telling yourself: (*a*) I'm an impatient mother, and (*b*) therefore, I'm a worthless, evil person. The first sentence may well be true, the second is totally false, and because you believe this nonsense you get depressed again whenever you are less than a perfect mother. Now prove to me that you are a bad person because you are a bad mother."

"Bad mothers are evil," she retorted.

"Who says so? You do, by your very definition. Bad mothers are inefficient and damaging to their children, true. Bad mechanics can cause accidents, and bad doctors can kill. Would you say everyone who isn't good at what he does is a worthless, good-for-nothing person?"

"Of course not, but that's different."

"It's not different. It's the same thing. In your case, however, you feel wicked because you don't have certain desirable mothering skills. You're simply choosing to become depressed over this fault rather than over your other weaknesses, such as being a poor bridge player or dancer. Yet some people blame themselves over those deficiencies."

"I don't care to be either of those. I want to be a good wife and mother."

"What about the woman who cheats on her husband and beats her children and doesn't mind doing either one of these things. Is she blameworthy?"

"Of course she is."

"But you just said that you're worthless only when you're poor at something you want to be very good at. According to your reasoning, a woman who doesn't want to be a good wife and mother should not blame herself any more than you should blame yourself for not being good at bridge or dancing."

For several moments she studied this remark.

"I confess that what you say sounds logical, but I somehow can't get myself to accept it."

"No doubt. I'd hardly expect you to throw your long-held ideas out of the window until you had thoroughly convinced yourself how wrong your present beliefs really are. It's going to take a lot of hard mental work on your part to straighten out the foolish notions you've revered all your life—ideas such as: that people are bad and should suffer for their wickedness; or, that you're nothing unless you're good at what you do. These superstitions have to go. They have caused you a great deal of grief. Give them up for the neurotic trash they are, and you'll really see for the first time in your life what real Christian peace of mind is like."

"Frankly, I feel unchristian, even sinful, contemplating *not* blaming myself for what I've done."

"What's so Christian about your tearing your heart out ten years after you've sinned? Is that the sort of peace of mind religion is supposed to bring? Would God or Christ want you to suffer as you have? Didn't Jesus tell the adulteress, "Go, and sin no more"? Notice, he didn't tell her to stop sinning and start hating herself."

"He wouldn't have approved of hate," she replied.

"Of course not, not to others and not to oneself. He even forgave his crucifiers. Doesn't that suggest that he felt all people were worthwhile?"

"Yes, it does. I wish I could be that way."

"You can if you'll only challenge those sick ideas of yours and see how wrong they really are."

"But, Doctor Hauck, most people believe them. You're the only one I've ever heard of who didn't think it was right to feel depressed over an awful deed."

"I can believe that, Mrs. Botin, though I'm by no means the only one who sees things this way. If there were more, we wouldn't have so many depressives and haters in the world. I'm afraid numbers is no argument. They're all wrong on this score and that's all there is to it. If they want to believe people should be perfect, or that hating oneself is a good way to change oneself, let them. I'll probably be seeing them next week. And if you ever want to stop being depressed, like it or not, you'll have to forgive yourself. That may be hard to do, but always remember, it'll be harder on you if you don't."

"What do you mean?"

"I'm referring to your emotional misery. There's nothing nice about that. If you don't work hard to control your self-blame, you'll pay the price of being depressed. What's so easy about that?"

"Nothing. It's terrible."

Her idea of being worthless unless she was perfect was never left unchallenged. Eventually, when she learned to accept herself, it was safe to advise her to tell her husband, who, incidentally, reacted extremely well. As she grew calmer she gained greater tolerance for her children, which gave her a new-found pleasure. She learned to enjoy them for the first time, something she could never do while using all her energies to loathe herself. Her attendance at church became more regular and was accompanied with a sense of joy rather than dread.

Depression and Conceit: Mr. Saley

It was commonly known that the depressed client has intense feelings of being inferior and worthless. To mention depression and conceit in the same breath, therefore, must seem like a blatant paradox. It will be seen on closer examination, however, that grandiosity, conceit, and unrealistically superior expectations are close relatives of depression.

Mr. Saley was acutely aware of his poor occupational performance over the past fifteen years. His high aspirations had not materialized and he was blaming himself severely for these failures. For a time I heard little else from him but how worthless he was, how he had let his family down, how he could not look people squarely in the eye, etc.

"Mr. Saley," I finally said, "you may be shocked by what I'm about to say, but if you give me a minute, I'll clarify my statement. You keep insisting on how good-for-nothing you are. You firmly believe you're bad, worse than most people, and a very inferior human being. Right?"

"That's about it."

"Now, what would you think if I told you that underneath this attitude you have some of the most superior notions about yourself that I've ever heard?"

"I'd say you were crazy," was his instant reply.

"I thought you'd say something like that. People like you are usually shocked to find out they think they're better than everyone else. Wait, let me finish before you protest again. I say you have superiority feelings because you think you must be perfect to be a decent citizen. You judge yourself by the harshest standards imaginable. Why do you do that? Obviously because you must believe you should measure up to some godlike standard. If you didn't think you were so much better than others, how could you be so mad at yourself when you fall short of your lofty goals? You don't get disgusted with other people when they act like mere mortals. But when *you* fail at something it's as if you were saying: 'It's all right for the other fellow. He's just a normal, average person. We can't expect much from trash like him. But me, if I did that, it would be a different story. I'm superior to him, so I can't be satisfied with the same standards he has.' "

"I don't believe I'm superior or anything of the kind. If I did, why would I feel so inferior all the time?"

"Because your superior expectations aren't being met. If you really believed you were as good as others, you'd accept yourself just as calmly as you accept others when they goof off badly. But you don't give yourself that break. You're being conceited to think that everything you do must be so much better than others and that you're a worse person than those who commit the same errors as you."

"I'd be quite content to be just average. I really don't need to be the best."

"That's what you say now. For fifteen years though you've been hating yourself whenever you acted just average and didn't advance as fast as you demanded. Then you became panicky and nervous, and this helped bring out more failure. If you had really not considered that being the best was such an important need, you wouldn't be talking to me now."

"I thought I was being reasonable with myself. I tried hard, had my setbacks like we all do, and then worked harder."

"And you hated yourself as well when you didn't perform perfectly. That's where your grandiosity and conceit come in. You believed that you, the mighty Mr. Saley, God's gift to the accounting field, had no business having a hard time meeting his goals. It's all right if those other peasants stumble along, falling short of their goals, but not you. Can't you see how a strong sense of superiority *must* underlie your thinking in order for you to feel disappointment as you do?"

"I confess I never thought of it like that. However, as you explain it, I must say it makes sense, even though I don't want to believe it. Apparently, then, I've been unreasonable with myself instead of too lenient, as I've always thought?"

"You can answer that better than I."

"Yes, I suppose I can. It's true I have always wanted to advance and be recognized for having been superior at something. But to say I have an underlying feeling of being better than others, I still can't accept that. The only feelings of myself that I've been aware of for a long time have been blaming ones."

"Don't think I expected you to go along with me right away. I want you to think over my statement very seriously and we'll discuss it again next week and see what you think about your grandiosity and conceit then."

Some time is usually required for the depressed client to gain the necessary insight to truly understand his unconscious conceit. The idea is so foreign to his normally hateful perception of himself that it really makes no sense to him initially.

One must be cautious not to show contempt in the use of words such as conceit, grandiosity, or superiority. The client is already blaming himself enough for his shortcomings. If we proceed to show disgust because of these underlying attitudes, he may very likely blame himself even more. Humor can again assist the counselor in helping his client swallow this bitter pill.

Depression and Self-pity: Mrs. Plaque

Along with guilt, self-pity is another common cause of depression. Since there is more than one etiological base for depression, the counselor should go to some pains to determine which type of depression he is dealing with. Unless he does so, he may make the mistake of treating all depressions alike. This would be folly.

To relieve a depression that results from self-blame and guilt, a very specific set of irrational ideas must be challenged. These ideas are not at all identical to the irrational ideas that create a depression that is characterized by self-pity. As we have shown, depression caused by guilt stems from Irrational Idea No. 2 (one must be perfect to be worthwhile) and Irrational Idea No. 3 (people are evil and should be severely punished). Depression caused by self-pity on the other hand arises from Irrational Idea No. 4—"the idea that it is awful and catastrophic when things are not the way one would very much like them to be"; and Irrational Idea No. 5—"the idea that human unhappiness is externally caused and that people have little or no ability to control their sorrows and disturbances." Together they operate to create feelings of despair, injustice, hopelessness, and inadequacy.

A young married female was referred by her family doctor and her minister because of a periodic despondency which lasted from Monday to Friday each week. Her husband, a traveling salesman, was home only from Friday evening to Monday morning. In his company she readily brightened up. But as soon as he left, the depressed mood settled like a fog.

"You're going to be very surprised, Mrs. Plaque, when I tell you your husband's traveling has nothing directly to do with your black moods. You're the one who is making you feel depressed all week."

"Oh, I know I make myself unhappy, but it's because I'm all alone except for our girl, Janie."

"Not quite. You're alone all week long. That's true. You're lonely perhaps. That's true too. It can't be those facts that are upsetting you. Only false things you believe can disturb you."

"Like what?" she asked, not appreciating my disagreement.

"Like, 'It's terrible to be lonely. It can't be tolerated. It'll kill me if I have to go through another week like the last one.' And so on. These are false ideas, and if you really believe them, you're bound to stay depressed either until you learn to question those beliefs or until your husband gets a job at home."

"It *is* terrible to spend every night and every day by myself with only a one-year-old to keep me company. I don't see how you can say it's any different."

"Suppose your husband drank and beat you up every weekend. How would you feel then about his being gone all week?"

"I suppose I might look forward to a little peace and quiet," she replied. "What does that prove?"

"That it is not your husband's absence that depresses you. It is your feelings of self-pity that make you miserable. You say on the one hand that you could tolerate being alone all week if your husband were mean to you, but you can't tolerate being alone if he's nice to you. Doesn't make much sense, does it?"

"Sure it does. If I didn't love Roger, I'd be happy to be alone."

"Wouldn't your frustrations be the same?" I asked.

"I suppose so, but they'd be easier to live with."

"Then you agree that your frustrations can be tolerated a great deal better than they are?"

"I'm afraid you have me there. In other words, if my situation would not change at home regardless of the kind of husband I had, it should be possible for me to accept it in either case."

"Most certainly. You'd still be alone. You'd still have only your youngster to talk to. You wouldn't have to like that, of course, but you could put up with it and make the most of it."

"And that's not what I'm doing now, is it?"

"Hardly. You're adding internal pain to external frustration."

"I'm making it twice as bad by getting depressed, is that it?"

"Of course. Stop and think which of these unpleasant things is really the greater. Is it more painful to be alone all week, or to be depressed all week?"

"That question never occurred to me. I guess I was assuming they had to go together."

"Exactly. You've noticed how I refer to each separately? That's because they are not directly connected as you've believed they are. For the time being you aren't able to do a thing about your husband's work. You can, however, do a great deal about how you react to his being gone. His absence is out of your control, but your depression is not."

"And what do I do to control these feelings?"

"Challenge those irrational notions I mentioned before and convince yourself how wrong they really are."

"Which notions were they?"

"First, the idea that unhappiness is externally caused and that you have little power over these feelings, and secondly, the idea that it is awful and catastrophic if things are not the way you want them to be. Fight those ideas constantly and you'll soon come out of your mood."

In following sessions she was asked to look at her situation differently and to count her blessings. Even though she might never relish having her husband be a traveling salesman, there were still some benefits she had overlooked among her circumstances.

5
Teaching the Unanxious Life

DEPRESSION AND GUILT, ANGER AND RESENTMENT, WORRY AND anxiety: these are the pairs of triplets that cause the majority of emotional problems. The pastoral counselor who can assist his clients in obtaining relief in all three areas can regard himself as quite accomplished. There are admittedly other areas of instruction in which it is very worthwhile to gain skill, such as sexual problems, poor self-discipline, and the rearing of children. However, if the minister has the foundations in counseling the depressed, the angry, and the fearful, he can use this knowledge to excellent advantage when dealing with related problems, since these same emotions often accompany the other disturbances.

Biblical Justification for the Unanxious Life

It is written, "This is the day which the LORD hath made; we will rejoice and be glad in it" (Ps. 118:24). How profound these few words are. How simply they ask us to live one day at a time, to make the most of the present. And by implication they urge us not to dwell exceedingly on the future or to ruminate over the past. Further, they tacitly recognize that each day *can* be enjoyed to some extent, regardless of what it brings. No suggestion is made that the day should bring gladness only if one does not experience a reversal or tragic happening. The gladness of this day is conditional upon no event. This day has much to offer. It can bring beauty and satisfaction to those who will see these twenty-four hours as an opportunity for self-fulfillment or for altruism. Because our days are numbered we are wisest when we use them to enhance life rather than to deny life.

Throughout the Gospels we find repeated reference to the expectation that man will and can find contentment and peace of mind on this troubled earth. "Let not your heart be troubled, neither let it be afraid" (John 14:27). This verse states the same viewpoint. It does not suggest that we be untroubled only under certain ideal conditions. It denies the necessity of fear, from whatever cause. The anxious soul has never truly understood the words from Matt. 6:25-26, which make the most unequivocal plea for the unanxious life: "Take no thought for your life, what ye shall eat. . . ." The most dreaded of human experiences, death and physical privation, are not excluded in this passage. They are to be faced with composure. This is a difficult task, but the ancients were most wise in thinking it attainable at all; not merely desirable, but possible.

Nor is fear itself to be feared. "Be not afraid of sudden fear, neither of the desolation of the wicked, when it cometh" (Prov. 3:25). Centuries later we have learned to appreciate this psychological tendency for man to worry over worry, to become anxious over anxiety, and to fear fear. This knowledge plays a particularly important role in RET's handling of anxiety reactions. It is essential for every minister who wishes to counsel the anxious to appreciate this fact.

The strongest belief in the unanxious life can probably be found in Phil. 4:11: "Not that I speak in respect of want: for I have learned, in whatsoever state I am, therewith to be content." Rational-emotive therapy makes the claim that frustration and emotional disturbance are two separate experiences and are furthermore not causal in relationship. Paul has shown the way, as have other ancient philosophers, to find contentment regardless of outer conditions. He further makes the point that his emotional control was a learned act, not a natural act, and he offers it to others as a reasonable style of life. Most importantly it should be realized that he too makes no exceptions: "in whatsoever state I am . . ." covers all human experiences, and mentions no exclusions. We rational-emotive counselors make the same claim: that this control is admittedly difficult to learn but nevertheless possible to attain, except under conditions of severe physical pain. It is not an outlandish notion concocted by foolish idealists, but rather a perfectly sound principle based on very extensive clinical data.

Our last quotation (these are only a few from many) expresses clearly how God regards fear. "God hath not given us the spirit of fear; but of power, and of love, and of a sound mind" (II Tim. 1:7). Even God rejects fear as an acceptable human standard. Power, love, and a sound mind are his gifts to man, and with them he expects us to rid ourselves of fear. Is the task of the minister different from that of the psychologist? Is not the removal of a phobia as much the mission of the minister as of the psychologist? Is not the removal of anxiety as much your concern as it is mine? I will presently demonstrate that anxiety is a special type of fear, nothing more. Therefore the pastor has, it seems to me, Biblical justification to remove this mental hazard wherever and whenever he finds it, for fear is an unholy, irreligious, and faith-defying attitude.

Theories of Anxiety

Probably no term in psychiatric nomenclature is as widely used and misunderstood as is anxiety. Prevailing views are frequently aligned, to be sure, but not totally in agreement. Goldstein[18] says that there is always one factor present among the many kinds of happenings that lead to anxiety—namely, the inability to stretch one's abilities to match one's demands on himself. Cannon[19] regards disturbed bodily homeostasis or threats to an imbalance of the homeostatic state as the cause of anxiety. Simpson[20] and Kierkegaard,[21] among many others, feel that anxiety is an inevitable feature of existence, closely related to man's biologic nature. They further suggest that anxiety is the sure knowledge of freedom as a possibility before that freedom has occurred. Freud [22] regarded unconscious conflicts as the primary motivation for anxiety. Sullivan[23] finds anxiety primarily motivated by the loss of security from disturbed interpersonal relationships. May[24] postulates anxiety to be due to experiencing the threat of nonbeing, the threat that one can become nothing.

We find some agreement among these views, but not sufficient to warrant a consensus. We shall presently see that another view of anxiety has emerged that adds to the debate on an already unsettled question: the view that anxiety is caused by an irrational belief.

RET differs with traditionalists also over the belief that anxiety has value and can be healthy. A number of thinkers hold this view quite literally. Menninger[25] refers to worry as an "earmark of civilization" but is cautious to distinguish this kind of concern from pathological anxiety, which is defined as worry about nothing, i.e., the unknown. Portnoy[26] speaks of a normal and neurotic involvement in anxiety. May[27] flatly contends that counseling's goal is not the elimination of anxiety, but the conversion of neurotic anxiety into more *normal* anxiety.

A third difference between rational-emotive counselors and others is over the distinction they make between fear and anxiety. Portnoy calls fear a peripheral threat that does not threaten one's sense of being. The danger is real, can be assessed, and can either be combated or retreated from. Goldstein feels that fear is the anticipation of nervous tension. Schneider[28] describes fear as that state which a person is able to act upon, whereas one is not able to act upon anxiety. Integration as a personality is still intact under fear but is not so under anxiety. Alexander and Ross[29] also connect fear with the possibility of external danger, while anxiety is uncontrolled sexual or aggressive drive stimulation. They thus distinguish between anxiety hysteria (in the case of sexual or aggressive drives) and superego anxiety, which refers to tension generated by the conscience.

Rational-Emotive Theory of Anxiety

Regardless of what the person's concern is, whether failure to live up to expectation, being overwhelmed by id forces, or the threat of nonbeing, in the final analysis it is his erroneous belief that he *must* be alarmed over these possibilities and never allow his thoughts a moment's diversion that causes anxiety. Here is the precipitate that is distilled from almost all the above theories. It is not what might happen to us, but rather our attitudes about these dangers that makes us anxious. This is true whether we have become tense over losing employment or over becoming anxious, for the latter is frequently such a concern that people make themselves anxious over its possible recurrence. Anxiety, then, according to our view, is the result of Irrational Idea No. 6—"the idea that if something is or may be dangerous or fearsome one should be terribly concerned about it and should keep dwelling on the possibility of its occurring." Accompanying this idea is a second, which often sets the worrying into motion: Irrational Idea No. 10—"the idea that one should become quite upset over other people's problems and disturbances." Once initiated by this belief, anxiety is maintained and even heightened by Irrational Idea No. 6. Rational-emotive counselors have demonstrated repeatedly that any event—failure, homeostatic imbalance, death, or any other tragedy—can be faced with equanimity if the individual strenuously challenges each of these neurotic beliefs. The greater the impending danger, the more effort he must expend in challenging these irrational ideas. But, if he does challenge them, the usual accompanying anxiety is diminished or even eliminated.

Furthermore, we do not regard anxiety as ever being healthy, although it may well be regarded as normal and natural in the statistical sense. The anxious individual can do no better at solving his dilemmas because he experiences these tensions than he can if he remains calm and rationally decides on a course of action. Anxiety inhibits action that might prove beneficial and easily builds little issues into big ones. Most pernicious is its tendency to produce and engineer the very situation it dreads. The schoolboy who worries over his oral report before the entire class may well become so fearful of doing badly that a smooth, well-delivered report is all but impossible. The driver who is nervous and tense because of one accident is likely to have another.

Any fearful event requires all the intelligent thought that can be applied to it. Any time spent on worrying is time not spent on resolving the problem or on learning to accept it. Practically speaking, one need not be unduly concerned over mild anxiety that does not hamper other constructive action. Nevertheless, it does not follow that even minimum anxiety is helpful toward the reduction of frustration. Frustrations themselves, by definition, provide sufficient displeasure to create a minimal but healthy state of tension to motivate persons into action. Tension differs from anxiety in that it is not a fear and is not always painful. When it increases to the point of pain it then becomes a neurotic affection that can be transformed into any of the common emotional reactions such as depression, anger, or fear.

Our last disagreement with traditional views of anxiety is with the distinction made between fear and anxiety. Traditionalists regard fear as something quite different from anxiety. The fact that the danger is known on the one hand and unknown on the other serves as a basis for this distinction. This is a sensible distinction, but it infers a greater degree of difference between these two states than there is. The distinction more sensibly suggests that anxiety is a special kind of fear, a fear of the unknown, and nothing more. The moment that the unknown is identified, the anxiety becomes a fear and can be eliminated as any fear or phobia can be. This is, in fact, the goal of the counselor—to help his client understand what he fears, to bring it into full awareness, and then to desensitize him to it. We cannot accept the view of the existentialists who insist that fear is only another emotion while anxiety is a threat to being (*Dasein*). This is not, according to them, equivalent to a fear of death, because death can be known, whereas for anxiety the fear is unknown.

A person can be anxious over dying, even if he does not know that he fears death; he can be anxious over leaving his home, even if he does not know that he fears that he will attack women. I prefer to think of anxiety as a fear of any event: nonbeing, death, failure, loss of employment, rejection, etc. This fear is anxiety if the event is not consciously recognized by the subject as being the phenomenon he dreads. When he verbalizes exactly what it is he dreads (and it could be the same events mentioned above), he might well appear clinically just as "anxious," but this should then be thought of as a fear. I know of no differences physically between a fear reaction and an anxiety reaction. The victim trembles for both, cold-sweats for both, is mentally preoccupied over both, loses sleep and appetite over both, etc. Therefore, we empirically conclude that all anxiety reactions are exactly the same as fears, the one difference being: the object of the fear is unknown.

A discussion of fear and anxiety is incomplete unless the concept of phobia can be logically distinguished from the former states. It too is a fear, but unlike anxiety, in which case the subject does not know what he fears, the phobic subject thinks he knows what he fears but is incorrect in this assumption. He has transformed the originally repugnant object into another form and thereby repressed the original object from his consciousness while gaining greater control over the symbolic object. A girl who actually fears her witchlike mother could gain in two ways by symbolically changing the mother into a cat. She can now deny the fear of the mother, and if careful, can easily avoid most cats.

It would be wrong to call this a fear, because it is not cats that she actually fears. It would also be wrong to call this an anxiety, because she thinks she does know what she fears. It deserves another name because it does not suit either of the two conditions above.

The counselor is cautioned to study the complaints of the client carefully if they involve the issue of a fear or its other two forms. As with depression and its three types, so with fear and its three types.

The singer who is nervous before a performance is experiencing fear. She fears performing badly and she *knows* it. The shopper who is suddenly seized with the need to get out of a crowded store is experiencing anxiety in all likelihood, but does not have a clear idea of what she fears. She does not know that being far from the entrance, it would be difficult for her to work her way through the mob if the tiny sensation of nervousness just experienced suddenly got out of hand and turned her into a raving madwoman. The girl who dreads insects, though she has never been bitten by one, *may be* experiencing a phobia. She thinks she actually fears insects but in reality she fears the guilty memory of her playmate's fingers as he played with her sexually when they were children.

It can readily be seen that a fear cannot be overcome unless the fear can first be identified. In the case of an anxiety attack or a phobia the counselor must help the client understand the true nature of his fear. If his complaints are vague, it can usually be assumed the client is afraid of being nervous. If his fear seems unreasonable and, in the mind of the counselor, could symbolize another fear, then this should be explored, brought to light, and regarded as a phobia.

Phobias, being relatively rare in comparison to fears and anxieties, will not be further elaborated upon.

Concern, Worry, Fear—A Continuum

Unfortunately these words are frequently used interchangeably. This is an unsound practice, because the counselor must have available to him words that do not convey sameness. We prefer, therefore, to use the term "concern" for that degree of regard for an issue which is relatively free of tension, and to reserve the terms "worry," "fear," and "anxiety," for those which are not free of tension. This is a perfectly valid distinction, since not all awareness of frustrations is unsettling. This distinction deserves to be made by the use of suitable terms.

Second along this continuum from indifference to panic is worry, that persistent, gnawing state which enters so many lives but does not incapacitate to the point of requiring professional help. Fear and its varieties (anxiety, panic, and dread), however, are so painful as to require relief from their unbearable tension.

How will the counselor know which state his client is experiencing? Might the client not say that he is concerned, when it is apparent that he is anxious? A simple approach is to ask the client how he feels. If he describes an unpleasant or painful state, he is worrying, at the very least, despite his assertion that he is only concerned. The degree of pain or discomfort measures (crudely, to be sure) how much he is worrying or being fearful. The point to bear in mind is that if he feels discomfort, he cannot be merely concerned. We must then show him that he is *over*concerned and that this will be injurious to him until he becomes *only* concerned. Case examples to follow shortly will bring out the significance of this distinction. Incidentally, the same care is taken to distinguish for the client the difference between wanting something (and being merely disappointed) and demanding something (and being angry). If he is angry, we can be certain he has *insisted* on his own way rather than preferred it, despite his claim to the contrary. Likewise, the person who insists that he was concerned, though not worried, over not getting a raise—but who at the same time reports discomfort in his stomach—must be shown what this means. The stomach pain means that he *was* worried and that he verbalized to himself thoughts that he does not realize and that are quite different from the thoughts he would have had if he were *only* concerned.

Fear as a Cycle

Rational-emotive psychotherapy has had better than normal success with anxiety states because it is very much aware of the cyclical nature of fear. At the risk of being momentarily redundant, let us study this phenomenon in more detail.

It is literally possible to be afraid of anything.[30] Though this comes as no surprise to most counselors, the fact does seem to escape them that after once having experienced the shattering tensions of fear, a person can tremble at the thought of experiencing fear. In other words, he can become nervous over the anticipation of becoming nervous; he can worry that he might worry.

This problem often originates with a significant environmental issue over which the client has disturbed himself. If this disturbance was in the form of excessive worry, he will very likely remember this uncomfortable period and worry himself over its return. In the meanwhile, the original traumatic problem may have disappeared but the nervousness remains. A new focus of preoccupation will have replaced the original one. Now, for example, he may have found a job, but he is tense and edgy lest he have a recurrence of that fearful feeling he had while unemployed. The counselor can easily be misled to believe that his client is worrying over being unemployed rather than over being *nervous* again.

A frequent companion to the fear of another attack of nervousness is the more dreaded fear that the victim will lose his mind. The fact that he may have been anxious for years and that he recovered after a thousand such brief attacks seems to offer little solace to the worrier, who is convinced that the next spell of anxiety will bring on insanity. The occasionally dramatic and tragic events in the news about ex-hospital patients going berserk plagues these people into believing they too will run amok "one of these times."

This fear of insanity must be shown to be an exaggeration. The anxious person is not truly likely to go berserk. That degree of disintegration is not usually part of the fear syndrome. In all likelihood the only thing that will happen to the anxious client the next time he goes through a "nervous reaction" is that he will sweat, shake, and feel awful for a time and then recover—this and *nothing* more. Ample proof can be given him for this by pointing to his history of this problem, and the fact that, were his tensions to lead to insanity, they probably would have done so before now.

A Case of Anxiety and *Fear: Mr. James*

The following encounter was with a twenty-seven-year-old married man, the father of two children, who had been married six years and who developed nervous symptoms a year ago.

"I can't get it out of my head that I might have another feeling like I had so many times before. It scares the pants off of me to even think about it," was his report. "And it usually gets worse when I'm out by myself."

"You mean you worry that you'll become shaky and the minute you worry, you *do* begin to feel nervous?"

"That's right. I feel like I want to jump right out of my skin just at the thought of going through that feeling again."

It is apparent that Mr. James knows what he is afraid of: nervousness. This is unusual insight, since many clients are unaware that this is their fear. Most counselors would regard this as a classical example of anxiety neurosis. Not so! He is aware of what scares him: "that feeling."

"Assuming you're right, Mr. James, that you might have another attack of nerves, why should you worry about it?"

"Because I can't stand it."

"But you *have*, many times. During the past year, haven't you had this feeling about once a week?"

"More than that. Sometimes several times a day."

"Then you must have gone through this nervous reaction hundreds of times during the past year. Doesn't that prove you can stand it?"

"It should, I suppose, but I dread it anyway."

"And that's why you have it so often. The more you

worry over feeling nervous again, the more likely it is you will make yourself nervous. It's your overconcern that you'll worry again that makes you worry again."

"I know that, doctor, but what can I do about that? I can't stop worrying. That's impossible."

"It's not impossible at all. Stop saying to yourself: 'Will I be upset today? It can't happen again. I've got to fight this thing. Man, it's terrible.' Instead, tell yourself: 'Maybe I'll get upset again today, but I'm not going to think about it. The more I stew over it, the quicker I talk myself into feeling tense. My worrying brings on these feelings, so relax.' Now if you talked like that to yourself, it would literally be impossible to become nervous again ever in your life."

"That sounds fine, doctor, but I think I'd only be whistling in the dark. I doubt that I could convince myself that what you're saying is true," he replied honestly.

"I agree. It wouldn't work if you weren't convinced you didn't need to be afraid of being nervous again. Why won't you convince yourself of that?"

"Well, everybody worries about awful things that might happen to them. It's natural."

"Yes, I agree it's natural to worry about some harmful event, but that still doesn't mean you have to. Be unnatural and you'll be better off. It's natural to get cavities, or to grow old and fat, but you brush your teeth, and that's very unnatural. People dye their hair and watch their diets so nature won't take its course. And aren't they better off for it?"

"What I'm doing then is natural? It's bad for me but normal?"

"Right. Millions of people are fearful, worried, or anxious all the time. But what good is it? Wouldn't they all be better off if they were calm, even if that were *not the normal* thing to do?"

"I suppose they would be. I still don't see how I can avoid getting tense by saying those things you mentioned, however."

"Just repeating my sentences won't do the trick, obviously. You have to question very seriously the philosophical belief behind your neurotic sentences. You believe falsely that people ought to worry and think endlessly about a tragedy or unpleasant event when it looks as if it might happen."

"I sure do."

"Why *should* you? Ask yourself *that* for a change. *Is* it really necessary and unavoidable to worry about something that might be dangerous? Where's your proof? For example, did you worry about being injured in your car on your way down here this morning?"

"No, but I get your point. I suppose I was in real danger, but I didn't let it bother me."

"That's the idea, Mr. James. You didn't talk yourself into a nervous state, although you could have. There are literally endless dangers around you all the time, to which you don't give two cents worth of worry. You take your chances at being held up on the street, or having an airplane land on you. They're real dangers but cause you only normal concern. This worry thing isn't any different. It's painful, to be sure, but no more dangerous or harmful than these other things that might happen to you. Still you insist you *must* worry about a small danger but not about a big one."

"Doesn't make much sense, does it?"

"No, it doesn't, Mr. James, and it never will. But you

won't see that until you decide to question that belief you hold, each and every time you notice you're worrying."

"Which belief is that?"

"The crazy notion that you should brood, worry, or always be overconcerned about becoming nervous simply because it's painful and could happen again. Show yourself by critical examination how irrational that idea is, and you can't possibly become so disturbed again."

Charged words such as "crazy" are used to good advantage by fulfilling the emotive side of this approach. They carry impact, honesty, and unforgettableness. Reasoning with him from a purely cold, logical, and neutral position would turn our session into an intellectual debate.

He reported moderate success with his anxiety during the next two weeks, but saw no change in his fear of going forth alone. When asked if he had been trying to be more aware of his thoughts prior to feeling shaky he reported: "I did think of something I haven't told you before, and I wonder if it explains why I'm afraid to be out by myself. I keep thinking something worse could happen to me once I got upset. You know, snap."

"You mean go insane?" I asked.

"Yeah, people can get so sick, can't they, that they flip their lids?"

His facetiousness was a thin mask covering a deep fear that he might go berserk, for did not his shattered nerves already suggest a dangerous loss of control? In addition to teaching him that worry is senseless, even over this possibility, the counselor is well advised to show him how far-fetched such an occurrence actually is.

I recapitulated an idea I had brought out before. "Sure you could lose your mind, but what are the odds? It certainly isn't very likely in terms of your history. Stop and think back a moment. Think of all the times you've been upset. After going through nervous attacks for several hundred times, don't you think it's time you concluded that nothing more than nervousness will happen to you?"

"You mean that I'll be nervous and nothing more?"

"Yes, exactly. If you were really the type to go berserk and run amok, don't you think it would have happened by now?"

"I'd sure like to think so. I admit the idea of hurting other people makes me sick. But suppose I do have that fear again. What do I do about it?"

"Go over all the evidence that's staring you in the face. Question the idea that just because you're tense you must also become a raving maniac. Stop and think of what happens each time you get tense, and how basically harmless you've been in that condition. After all, the worst that's happened to you during one of these spells is that you shake, sweat, feel afraid and very uncomfortable; and *that's all.* In a matter of minutes or hours (seldom longer), you're composed again until the next episode."

"I suppose you're right. That *is* all that's ever happened when I got to worrying."

"Okay then, Mr. James, the next time you feel yourself slipping into one of these things, tell yourself calmly: 'Here's my old friend again. It's going to be rough for a little while, but if I don't get upset about anything else, it'll pass soon, as it always has. I'll just pace the floor for a while. That's all.'

"Don't tell yourself upsetting thoughts like: 'Great God, am I losing my mind? I'm going to lose control of myself this time, I just know it. I'd better fight this and worry, or who knows what will happen?' Thoughts like that will only make the nervous attack last longer than it would otherwise."

In the following weeks he reported some progress over the control of his numerous nervous episodes. The fear of being out alone, however, did not diminish, and now it began to appear to be a case of anxiety, not fear. He was repeatedly encouraged to examine his thoughts prior to these attacks in the hope that we could eventually learn what it was he feared. In his sixth session he finally supplied the answer: he feared striking up an acquaintance with a female and letting the friendship blossom into an affair. Apparently he had good cause. He was a handsome fellow who had had a full and varied sex life before marriage, and even carried on two affairs after marriage. One evening, about a year before entering counseling, he was in a café with his then-current mistress when he spotted his wife walking past the front window. She did not notice him, but his detection was so close that he realized the full impact of the position he had put himself in. There was no doubt in his mind that his marriage would be finished if his wife ever found him out, and from that one incident he realized how risky such conduct was. Thereafter he consciously decided not to continue these affairs and he held to his resolve. Shortly after making this decision, he showed the signs of anxiety he had described during his first interview. He apparently did not realize that his desire for a flirtation was still strong and might tempt him into an unwise move. More accurately, the cause of his distress was his fear that the temptation for an affair would be overpowering and that it had to be controlled by completely avoiding being out in the evening by himself.

Once experienced, this *anxiety* (fear) became the cause for a second fear—that he would become tense and upset again at any moment. This explained why he was often distressed when he was not tempted. His fear of insanity represented his concern that the secondary or derived fear would get completely out of hand.

The pastoral counselor would probably pounce on his sinful acts in the hope that with enough guilt, Mr. James would desist from such behavior in the future. This would be a mistake. First, if successful, the guilty Mr. James might develop a depression. If made to feel sufficiently guilty, he might even imagine a need for severe punishment for his evil ways. This would most easily be satisfied by having another affair, one that could readily be detected and bring on a swift divorce.

What is a conscientious minister to do? Can he be helpful to his client and still be true to his moral principles? He can. It depends upon whether his concern is changing Mr. James's behavior, or wanting him to suffer for his sins *as well* as to reform.

Mr. James regarded his liaisons as being risky rather than morally wrong. Such explanations are rightfully unsatisfying to the clergy. Ideally they would want him to understand the basic wrongness in his actions. Well and good. Let us see how Mr. James faced that issue as well as his fear of being tempted.

"First, Mr. James, I want to compliment you on that fine piece of detective work you did. It sounds very logical to me and I think you're on the right track. Secondly, why in the world do you have to be afraid you're going to seduce every other female you meet just because it sounds like an enticing idea?"

"I get pretty tempted sometimes, especially when I sense they want me to make a play for them."

"So you get tempted. So what? You're still not answering the question of why you think you can't keep yourself from doing something, merely because you'd like to do it very much."

"I suppose it's just normal to do things you think you'd like."

"I know, but that hardly means you have to give in to each and every impulse you get. You have impulses and urges all the time that you control beautifully, and some of those impulses could lead to serious consequences if gratified. In those cases, however, you're not telling yourself it's awful or terrible not to get what you want, but in the case of these women you are saying just that. And the more you upset yourself over not getting a woman, the greater the desire becomes, until you're so upset you really can't control yourself."

"I know exactly what you mean. Sometimes I'd be thinking about a certain girl so much she'd be on my mind all the time, and then I suppose I thought I'd die if I couldn't meet her."

"And it's all because you're always telling yourself that not having her would be the end of the world, which is a lot of nonsense; or that you ought to worry your fool head off over the possibility of making another date. I repeat, the more you worry yourself sick, the more you weaken your control over the very thing you're worried about."

Emotive expressions like "lots of nonsense," "your fool head," etc., should always be employed liberally to help a client move from his mental position. Reason needs the assistance of forceful language to dislodge the client from his present philosophical base and urge him to think along new lines.

Notice how Irrational Ideas 4 and 6 have been described without being specified as such.

He continued: "This temptation is really very different from others I've had. There wasn't as much at stake before."

"Wasn't there? Haven't you ever wanted to kill someone, or suddenly wanted to run over a pedestrian?"

"Not that I know of."

"I doubt that. Even so, I'm sure you've had the urge to steal something, maybe a car or an item in a store. That could get you into very serious trouble."

"Can't say that I ever felt that way either."

"You mean to say that you never wished you could pick up a television set and walk home with it, or to reach into a jewelry counter and grab a handful of diamond rings?"

"Oh sure, but I never took those thoughts seriously at all."

"That's what I mean. You had the thought all right, but you tossed it out of your mind. You could do the same with wanting to sleep with a certain girl too, couldn't you?"

"According to what you just said, I should be able to."

"You can. Just try to remind yourself how you control your urges every day and that the urge to date another woman is no different. It's just an impulse which you don't need to gratify even though you'd like to. Ever feel like telling your boss off?"

"Sure."

"Did you do it?"

"No."

"Ever get tired of company and want to tell them to go home?"

"Yes."

"Did you?"

"No, but I sure felt like it sometimes."

"Now, Mr. James, how is it you could control your impulses in all these instances and a thousand more I could name, but you can't control the impulse to set up an affair?"

"When you put it that way, it sure doesn't sound so frightening. I suppose I could control my talking to a girl if I can do all those other things."

"Wait a minute. Now you're overdoing it. Just because you badly want to avoid an affair hardly means you can't talk to a strange woman. You see how you're regarding yourself as a helpless victim of some all-powerful urge? Are you really in such danger if you strike up a conversation?"

"That's how they all start," he replied.

"Sure they do, but that's only the first of many steps before you're in bed together. It takes time for an affair to develop. You would need to meet the girl a number of times in all probability to arouse strong feelings in her for you. This in itself would probably require anywhere from a few days to several months. Don't tell me that in that time span you couldn't ask yourself whether you *needed* this affair and put a halt to it anywhere along the line? And even if you met someone who might join you in bed that very night, you'd still have hours at your disposal from the time you met her to the very moment you got undressed, during which you could talk yourself out of the affair."

"I see what you mean. That wouldn't really be anything to be frightened of, would it?"

"Right, Mr. James. Just don't get nervous or panicky if you happen to slip and start flirting. At that point you're still plenty safe. But if you start to build that slip into a big thing in your mind, you'll have it on your brain day and night. You will feel compelled either to give in to the desire, or to protect yourself from the temptation by this screwy scheme of insisting that you, a grown man, can't step out of the house by yourself."

"That's right, doctor. I was just thinking how I've sometimes had the urge to slip a few small items in my pocket at the supermarket. If I had gotten panicky over that possibility, I would have been scared of ever shopping again, wouldn't I?"

"Of course. It's not the urge that scares you. It's the way you convince yourself that because you have the urge, you're absolutely going to act it out. Rubbish."

Over the following weeks our interviews repeated essentially the same elements described. He still became tense at odd moments, still had flashes of dread that he would lose his mind, and still wanted company when he went anywhere in the evenings or weekends. Gradually, however, as he learned to challenge his irrational ideas more convincingly, he gained greater composure and peace of mind.

The Moral Question

Mr. James's symptoms subsided mainly because he was convinced that his impulses were controllable. Though this is a sufficient reason to consider the matter closed, it does not obviate the use of other logical arguments if such are available. In this instance there was another weapon we had at our disposal which, combined with the first insight, gave him additional protection against having future extramarital affairs: the moral issue.

I began one of our later sessions with: "Well, it seems as though you've mastered your problem quite nicely, Mr. James. I'm delighted for you. Do you think you'll be troubled by the fear of giving in to that impulse anymore?"

"I certainly hope not. Now that I see what I was afraid of and realize through our talks how foolish it is to think I'm going to do everything that comes into my mind, I have to laugh at how nutty I must have acted."

"Fine. And if you keep on thinking clearly, you should hardly ever be troubled this way again. Just to make certain, however, I want you to solidify your progress with one more change of attitude."

"Oh? What's that?"

"Getting you to see that having an affair is morally wrong. Now I don't mean that you are bad or wicked, only that your affair was. I'm glad you weren't crucifying yourself over it, because that would have made you anxious *and* depressed. By not blaming yourself for it you cut your problem in half."

"That's right. I was only afraid of what getting caught would do to my marriage, not that stepping out was itself so bad. These days it's getting to be pretty common, isn't it?"

"I'm afraid it is. That still doesn't make it morally right, however. You've been taught that by your church, I'm sure. Perhaps you ought to have a few talks with your minister. He could refresh your memory on the church's position in this matter. However, whether you do or not,

I'd like you to consider your adultery as an act of unfairness, even if you don't think of it as a sin."

The minister will perhaps protest this failure to equate unfairness with sin, and rightfully so. However, we do not want to enter theological polemics at this point but simply to discuss unfair behavior as an unethical act, unencumbered by complex religious questions.

He answered: "Yeah, I suppose it was. It turned out all right though. No one got hurt."

"That's just a lucky coincidence, Mr. James. You could just as easily have been detected or gotten your girl friend pregnant. Stop and think how that would have affected you, your wife, and your children."

"I know," he answered softly.

"Even leaving these obvious arguments aside, there is another point you should consider. You treated someone as you wouldn't care to be treated yourself: you broke your word. You promised to be faithful and you weren't. Can you see how any kind of stable living among people would be impossible if everyone did that? Unless you can okay adultery for your wife, you have no legitimate right to carry on an affair either. Otherwise you're saying that you're superior to her and you are guided by one standard but she is guided by another."

He agreed in principle but excused himself on the grounds that the double standard was an accepted norm of social conduct in our society. I insisted that this made no difference and gave an example to clarify my position.

"Suppose all the foremen in all the printing rooms in this city allowed all employees over six feet tall to have an hour for lunch and all the others, including you, only a half hour. Would you approve of that double standard?"

"Certainly not. But let's be realistic. They would never

do that only because the man was over six feet tall. They might do it because the six-footers worked harder and so deserved a longer rest."

"Now wait a minute, Mr. James. You're not talking about a double standard any longer. If they got a longer lunch period because they worked harder, then presumably you could work harder too and enjoy a longer lunch. The rules would apply not just to six-footers but to hard workers, which you could be if you wanted. In the matter of a double standard in sex, you're advocating that men *because* they're men should have greater freedom than women. That's just as unfair as it would be if a man's lunch period were determined by a factor other men could do nothing about. I don't see how you can okay an arbitrary rule in one case and not in another. Your position is indefensible and you know it. However, because it favors *you*, you've chosen not to question it seriously and deny yourself that advantage."

This kind of blunt and direct remark, which does not ask him if this is what he believes—it tells him—is highly recommended when rapport is firmly established.

"And then there's the whole question of going back on your word. When you were married, the two of you agreed to several things in addition to loving, honoring, and cherishing each other. For example, she's counting on you being disease-free and having a safe sex life. She's expecting your earnings and time to be spent on behalf of the family, not strangers. And she's expecting all your children to be hers. These conditions are taken for granted and are separate from the vows you took."

"How's that?" he asked.

"Because a man can love, honor, and cherish his wife and still love, honor, and cherish someone else. As long as his wife doesn't know about the other woman she can't order him to stop and make him keep his vow to honor her. That's the trouble with this secret stuff. The mate doesn't often find out about it until it's too late."

"You think a guy should go and tell his wife he's having an affair?" was his almost snide remark.

"I think he ought to call off his marriage if that's what he wants to do. It isn't immoral to change one's mind. It is immoral not to tell your mate, if that's what you've done."

"Why should that make all the difference?"

"Because you wouldn't be lying about honoring conditions that you are no longer honoring. It's just as if your boss let you come to work for a month and didn't tell you that you were fired four weeks before."

"I see your point. He has a perfect right to fire me but not to keep that to himself and let me work a month for nothing."

"Sure, it's keeping that knowledge away from you that constitutes the immorality."

"That's right. In other words, I *could* date again but I'd have to tell my wife our original agreement was off—that is, divorce her—and then I'd really be behaving fairly, wouldn't I?"

"Yes, as long as divorce didn't violate your moral and religious beliefs."

"Being Catholic, I'm afraid it would be out of the question. Anyway, I never considered divorcing my wife. I've loved her right through this mess of mine. It's just that I wanted her and some fun on the side too. You know the old saying about eating your cake. Incidentally, I wonder now if I didn't think what I was doing was really all right because I knew I didn't want to get rid of my wife. Perhaps, because I thought I was being so proper by loving her all along as I promised, I thought it wasn't so bad to carry on with others. Actually I would have been more decent to end the marriage if I thought I had the grounds and the approval of the church, and then become interested in any woman I liked. And if I couldn't have that approval, then I should simply have stayed by my word and been faithful."

"True, breaking your trust was the important point. Think this whole thing out very clearly, Mr. James, and I'm certain you'll be in better control of yourself."

6
Teaching Love and Forgiveness

AT A TIME IN HISTORY WHEN THE PREVAILING ATTITUDE TOward one's enemies was to hate them and cause them great harm, it was a miracle that a voice arose and spoke these beautiful words, "But I say unto you, 'Love your enemies, bless them that curse you, do good to them that hate you, and pray for them which despitefully use you, and persecute you'" (Matt. 5:44). Here is only a fragment of Christ's teachings, which has the power to instill love and forgiveness if it is faithfully followed. His message of love is central to the entire Christian ethic.[31] He concerned himself with it to his last breath. "Forgive them, for they know not what they do." Throughout the Gospels we encounter again and again his pleas for us to love one another and to forgive our trespassers. And still, the sincerest of Christians (ministers not excluded) have their angry and hateful episodes, many of them, sometimes daily or weekly. It is impossible to estimate how often people of good intent and strong religious persuasion allow themselves to be grudging, bitter, resentful, spiteful, angry, or hateful. Of all the emotions we as professionals must deal with, none are as frequent as the unloving and unforgiving. Why is this?

"According to your faith be it unto you" (Matt. 9:29).

This is the method advised to make Scriptures applicable to our daily lives. Those fortunate souls who listen and *believe* are blessed. Regrettably, many of us, because of our human frailties, want to have faith, but cannot have it through sheer will power. We require knowledge of a process. We ask the questions How? and Why? which have always plagued the curious. The Bible simply does not answer these queries in sufficient detail to enable any but the saintly to love their enemies without being shown the way. The gospel has been preached for so long that by now violence should have been erased from most areas of the world—*if* the appeal to faith were effective. Considering the centuries during which he has labored to bring his flock peace of mind, the Christian pastor should by now have emptied every state hospital and driven practically every mental health clinician out of business—*if* the appeal to faith were effective. Considering how long he has taught the commandment "Thou shalt not kill," he should have ended the last war almost two thousand years ago—*if* the appeal to faith were sufficient.

The simple truth of the matter is not that the Bible set impossible goals, but that it failed to offer more than faith as a means of achieving its ends. The problem is man's. Man must be shown how to accomplish these spiritual objectives by means *other than faith.* The remarks that will follow presently will attempt to accomplish this. I will endeavor to illustrate how it is literally possible to love one's enemies, to return good for evil, and *never* to bear a grudge.

Righteous Anger

The pastor may protest that this is an extreme position and makes no allowance for righteous anger (which one permits oneself to experience without guilt). This is not a valid criticism for three reasons: (1) *all* anger is righteous; (2) the Gospels refuse to make this concession; and (3) whether "righteous" or otherwise, anger of *any* kind, employed habitually, creates harmful, not beneficial, effects.

1. From the frame of reference of the individual who is angry, that anger is always justified. Unless he were already convinced of this, it would actually be impossible to *feel* anger. The emotion arises in the first instance because the subject is absolutely convinced of his rightness and the other's wrongness as well as of his right to punish the wrongdoer. An adolescent who answers his mother freshly because he was asked to take out the trash has as much righteous anger as his mother will have over the insult. Either party could easily make a case for himself if asked by a neutral person. Anger can only lack the conviction of righteousness when it is feigned, for instance, as by an actor. In that event it is only a pretense of an emotion.

An individual cannot pass lightly over his anger by insisting that it is harmless if he really loves the person at the same time that he is angry with him. This may indeed be true, but getting the target of his anger to understand that he is loved is another matter. Children find this a particularly impossible task. When criticized angrily, they will almost invariably assume it is they as well as their behavior which are under attack and tend to take all such remarks in a very personal way.

Indeed, many adults cannot separate vitriolic remarks aimed at their actions from personal references. It is a rare minister who can calmly regard his wife's disapproval of his many evenings away from home as only a criticism of his schedule. More than likely he will feel it as a personal assault, even if his wife should not intend it to be. Knowing how to make this distinction is a difficult skill for adults to master, to say nothing of what it is for children. The gist of the matter simply comes to this: if we are displeased with the *conduct* of others, we must express that fact calmly or it will not be believed. Becoming emotional over the issue invariably will be interpreted as displeasure with the person as well. The former approach will convince the wrongdoer that we still love him though we are displeased, while the latter convinces him that our love is suspended until the wrongdoing is corrected.

2. The references in the Gospels which speak so beautifully the message of love and forgiveness are numerous and almost perfectly consistent. Those who would make reference to Christ's driving out the money changers as evidence of his anger must be cautious in this interpretation. The books of Matthew, Mark, and Luke speak merely of Jesus firmly driving out the merchants and explaining his reasons for so doing. They make no reference to his being hateful or angry while ejecting them. Indeed, his words from Matt. 5:44, "Love your enemies . . . pray for them . . . which persecute you," would be hypocritical if we regarded this event in any other light.

The reference in Mark 3:5 to Christ's looking angry at those who were waiting to see if he would perform a miracle on the sabbath does not weaken this stand. Scripture does not say he *felt* angry, and certainly nothing in his consequent behavior would indicate that he experienced this emotion. He calmly proceeded to do a good deed, sabbath or no.

In a similar manner, reliance on other passages as evidence that he was capable of hatred is open to question. In Luke 17:3 he said: "Take heed to yourselves: If thy brother trespass against thee, rebuke him; and if he repent, forgive him." But he in no way implied that to rebuke meant to become angry with or to disapprove of one's fellowmen. This term can be understood to mean the same censure that we give our children for their many faults.

As I am not a scholar of the Bible, I cannot ignore the possibility that somewhere, unknown to me, are clear passages stating that Christ felt righteous anger. However, even if such "proof" should be forthcoming, I cannot conceive that Christ would have hate or anger for the person whose actions he was correcting. To believe that this is possible is to cast serious doubt on the sincerity and feasibility of the entire Christian belief: goodness over evil, love over hate, forgiveness over revenge.

We may either assume that the art of interpretation was lacking when it chose the particular English words with which we are familiar, or that Jesus, who suffered the pains inherent in a human body, also possessed some of the same personality frailties that we are subject to. Herman[32] has seen the heart of this issue by placing forgiveness as the focal point of the Christian movement. This writer regards God's full forgiveness of each and every one of us, regardless of our sinful, erring nature, *before* we utter a single word of confession, as the hallmark of our religious movement. To comprehend this fact and still to argue for righteous anger is folly.

3. Relatively little is written on the subject of the consequences of anger as compared to the endless attention paid by the analysts to depression and anxiety. Yet anger is probably far more frequent an emotion than the other two combined. We can safely establish this fact empirically by noting how frequently children quarrel with one another, by noting how often mothers and fathers are angry with their children or with each other, or by observing the many neighborhood, office, or relational disputes. The shapes of anger are endless; it appears in various guises, from kindness to outright violence. Between these poles we have all grades of grudging, resentment, bitterness, etc. The most frequent expression of anger is verbal argument, sometimes followed closely by physical punishment. Anger is the embodiment of everything that Christianity does *not* stand for. To experience anger and to believe that one is a follower of Christ is a logical contradiction. This then, from a theological reference, is the most significant consequence of anger.

Psychologically and medically speaking, however, anger has three prime effects: (*a*) it is self-damaging, (*b*) it indirectly generates more emotional disturbance, and (*c*) it is responded to with further misdeeds. (The second and third effects are not identical.)

Whatever harm we succeed in wreaking on others because of our own angry state is only part of the total harm achieved. There is the all-too-easily-forgotten damage imposed upon the inflicter by his own wrath. It is not possible to be angry with impunity except when that anger is mild. In all other instances, wrath takes its toll on the avenger as the parasite does on its host. Whether it be a mild loss of appetite or dangerously high blood pressure, anger brings pain. Anger cannot be enjoyed unless the person has such guilt that he welcomes this pain as penance. There are those who advocate the release of anger, rather than its suppression, and who show evidence of how "clearing the air" is personally very relief-giving. They forget that such explosive episodes are preceded by the discomfort of increasing anger until a point of eruption is reached. They are referring, not to the pleasure in feeling anger, but in *getting rid* of it. Not until the human system is emptied and done with this emotion is comfort regained. And this is identical to our original position: having anger is painful, while not having it is pleasant.

In truth, it must be granted that mild anger is harmless to its host and can be tolerated for a lifetime without serious consequences. But anger, of whatever degree, is an emotional habit, a way of life, and will find expression not only in conjunction with mild frustration but most certainly also with strong frustration. The latter will surely lead to drastic reactions: to hatred and violence, if expressed, and to migraine headaches or other psychosomatic complications, if unexpressed. How much better it would be to eliminate this emotion!

As we care most for those who are closest to us, it follows that they can frustrate us greatly and frequently. By dealing with these loved ones through the devices of scorn, ridicule, sarcasm, and disapproval, we encourage them to devalue themselves until they feel so inferior and wicked that change for the better is out of the question. With children and passive adults the voice of righteous anger speaks with the roar of authority. A parent who repeatedly excoriates his academically failing son should not be surprised when his son, who learns to regard himself as a hopeless dunce, continues to fail. It would be a miracle if the boy gained more self-confidence after frequent verbal blisterings. He would lose not only in self-confidence but also in self-respect. After his initial anger subsides, the youngster would experience guilt over disappointing his father and supposedly upsetting him as well. The end result is an unhappy person, well on his way to a neurotic existence. Much of the mental disturbance seen today is the result of this "corrective" approach.

Another frequent consequence of anger is its unerring ability to teach the victim to respond in kind and then righteously go out of his way to commit further misdeeds in the belief that revenge is sweet regardless of the personal harm to be suffered. Also, it teaches him that, being a black sheep, he has no choice but to behave as one. Those who practice anger fail to realize that their example is a great teacher, aside from being a great frustration. They are angry because frustrated, yet are insulted by a response of anger when *their* victims are frustrated. They can justify feeling that they have a greater right to be indignant only by neurotically believing that their wishes are always more important than anyone else's.

Inefficient is a good word to describe this sorry process. Without realizing it, or perhaps without even caring, the angry person often creates more of the very thing he wants so much to be rid of. And finally, the more his neurotic efforts are repaid, the more cutting, demeaning, and cruel he becomes. And so begins that tragic spiral, ever descending into the depths of hate until the absurd is accomplished: a beloved wife is shot by her husband during an argument over a lost trinket.

Anger has its specific internalized thoughts that trigger it into motion. When frustrated, the normal first response of the victim is to *wish* the event had not happened. He says to himself something like this: "I wish you'd stop yelling at me," or "I want you to love me," or "I prefer that you arrive on time."

Being wishes, their fulfillment is not a critical issue, not a catastrophe, not life or death. They are identical to the sort of wishes we have all had: "I want to be rich," or "I would like to be a movie star," or "I prefer a limousine to that jalopy." When not granted the riches, stardom, or new car, we accept the frustration gracefully, experiencing little more than a twinge of regret or a mild sense of disappointment. Desires, wishes, wants, and preferences are healthy expressions of our goals, and the failure to materialize these goals does not disturb us seriously or painfully.

It is commonly the second response to frustration that brings forth anger. The victim now unconsciously or consciously verbalizes: "Because I want you to stop yelling, you *must* stop yelling." "Because I want you to love me, you *have to* love me." "Because I desire that you arrive on time, you *should* arrive on time." The transformation is almost complete: the wish has become a demand, the preference has become a need, the desire has become a necessity. But notice how the perception of the frustration itself has altered. From an annoyance with yelling has sprung the belief that it is unbearable; the irritation with being unloved is now seen as a crisis; and the harmless act of being late is regarded as a catastrophe. It is this mental transformation from wishes to demands—the illogical belief that because we want things our own way, they *must, should,* and *ought* to be our way—that creates anger, resentment, bitterness, and hatred. It is no different from what the child thinks when he has a tantrum. The psychology of it is basically identical. Anger is anger, whether in a child or adult, and for the same general reason: the person wants something and believes he must have it. *All* anger can be accounted for in this way. Is it any wonder that Christ could not lower himself to it?

The Control and Elimination of Anger

The popular methods of dealing with anger fall under four headings: (1) removing the frustration, (2) suppression through willpower, (3) insight, and (4) ventilation.

It should be quite obvious why removing a frustration will practically always achieve a reduction of anger. When active children become quiet before a television set and cease their rowdiness, the harassed and angry mother will quickly become calm because the frustration is over. When an unkind remark has been apologized for, the offended person regards the frustration as ended. As it is his belief that the frustration was the literal cause of his resentment, it is consistent for him to believe its cessation will terminate the anger. In a manner of speaking this is true, but not for the reasons he believes. In reality, his *verbalizations* (which follow the ending of the frustration) are what reduces the negative feelings. When these attitudes do not change with a change in the situation, the emotion does not change either. We have all experienced a lingering hatred toward someone who offended us, even though he did his best to undo his original damage.

The second common method for controlling anger, suppression through willpower, is less effective but possibly more often employed. It is equivalent to counting to ten or biting one's tongue to prevent the explosive force of anger from erupting. Willpower is the agent used to keep the lid on these boiling passions. How unfortunate it is that this wonderful device is not employed to eliminate the anger rather than merely to control it. Over an extended period of time these suppressed forces manifest themselves in the many psychosomatic symptoms we have all become familiar with, two typical ones being high blood pressure and migraine headaches.

There are two other common methods of dealing with anger. The pastor will surely want to know what value insight and ventilation have in the matter of anger, since these are time-honored techniques. The former is particularly the choice of Freudians and Rogerians, while the latter is so natural to human nature as to be called a folk remedy.

The third common method of controlling anger is insight. Traditional therapists have considered anger to be of two kinds: justified and unjustified. The anger "aroused" by an obvious frustration, for example, was considered a reasonable reaction, hardly calling for correction. The man who becomes incensed over an insult is regarded as being of good character and quite right to become angry. It is a conscious act and holds no mystery. Should this man show anger and hostility to remarks made in good faith, however, the observation would be made that his anger is unreasonable, is caused by unknown facts, and could be eliminated upon the uncovering of these unconscious forces—upon the achievement of insight, in other words. Most therapists are quite adept at this kind of treasure-hunting in the mental world and in a reasonable number of visits give the client this much-needed insight. If the anger dissipates, insight or the transference experience with a benign counselor are credited with the success.

It is our steadfast position that this is an incomplete

understanding of this event. We believe it is not the insight or transference experience that changes the hostility to love. Rather, what causes the change is the cognitive process that takes place *after* the insight has been gained. The subject has learned, let us say, that he is habitually on the hostile and defensive side in his interpersonal relationships because his family has always been prone to find fault, and that he expects the same behavior from his adult social world. In and of itself this knowledge will not help him avoid defensiveness in the future. Unless he uses it to reason differently than he has in the past, it will simply remain an interesting bit of information, nothing more.

For the insight to be of value to him, he must draw from it conclusions such as the following: "Oh, I see now why I'm always ready to fight everyone I meet. I keep mistaking them for my family. That's silly. Others are not going to treat me the same way my folks did, although some might from time to time. Perhaps I'm getting some of that hostility because I enter most relationships expecting to be hated and then I act mean and defensive before I even know for sure whether or not that person is anything like my folks. Maybe if I stopped and judged each person carefully first before deciding offhandedly that he will for certain try to hurt me as my family liked to do, I'll get along a lot better and only be angry on rare occasions. Come to think of it, do I really have to be sore and defensive toward someone just because he doesn't like me?"

Although it appears that changes occurred after insight, closer analysis shows that a mental process similar to the above has quietly and unnoticeably taken place. Emotional relief follows from *this* step rather than the first. Only after such evaluative use is made of insight is the reduction of anger possible.

The fourth popular method of dealing with anger is ventilation. Everyone has used displacement as a quick source of relief for his hostile feelings. The slamming of a door, chopping of wood, taking a long walk, expressing oneself vituperatively—these are all means of ventilating anger once aroused. They are regarded as harmless, even healthy means of "letting off steam." They are feelings that could be dangerous if not allowed release.

It cannot be denied that there is much truth in this observation. At the same time it has been overlooked that ventilation of feelings, whether expressed verbally or physically, presupposes the creation of anger in the first place and then asks it to be continued needlessly. To get rid of anger through ventilation, it (the anger) must be experienced, tolerated a while longer as it becomes *augmented,* and finally expressed. There is danger in this. How much better to reverse angry feelings as they arise, to reduce them immediately, not through their release but rather through a conviction that they are *unnecessary* and needlessly self-induced. Ventilation often leaves a residue of the hatred, while reasoning can wipe it out completely.

The Avoidance of Anger

Before RET, dealing with hostility through these four methods was regarded as fully acceptable. Mental health workers simply did not consider its avoidance possible. They were taught that frustration invariably leads to aggression.[33] They totally ignored the Biblical injunction to return good for evil or to love one's enemies, probably because these sounded more like lofty ideals than attainable realities. Yet the control of anger by avoidance of anger is possible to an astonishing degree for those who have been taught the proper thinking skills. The only factor that prevents man from never experiencing anger is his infernal fallibility as a mortal. Within that limitation he can, with great effort, learn to be loving and forgiving ninety percent of the time. Some few saintly and exceptional persons may, for all intents and purposes, master this negative force so well that it could be said of them that they were never angry, resentful, or bitter again in their whole adult lives. Is this farfetched? Then consider that most of us will never as long as we live succumb to a number of passions such as murdering another human, although the human race will most certainly continue to do so. I believe we can approximate the same degree of control over anger that most of us have achieved over murder. Of course, it will take a long time.

Anger can be eliminated by the following three steps. First, the moment anger is felt, we must realize that the frustrating person, thing, or event has no direct relationship to this feeling, but rather that it is what we are telling ourselves about these circumstances that is angering us. Second, we must realize that we have mentally converted our wishes into demands, and that it is this conversion that makes up the subject matter of our internal verbalizations in step one. And third, we must question whether we really have a legitimate right always to be spared frustration, or to demand that other people should be infallible because we dislike fallibility.

It is this last step that is so difficult to master, because it involves the overthrow of long-standing attitudes of man's evil nature and his need to be treated harshly for his wrongdoings. Be that as it may, anger will never die within the human breast until these demands for perfect behavior are given up totally and without reservation. A profound philosophical change in beliefs that will grant humans the right to their God-given, imperfect, nature, and the conviction that we do not *need* to be pleased are the *only* ways to eliminate anger from the human repertoire.

More precisely, anger is related to the following irrational beliefs: Irrational Idea No. 3—"the idea that certain people are bad, wicked, or villainous and that they should be severely blamed and punished for their villainy"; Irrational Idea No. 4—"the idea that it is awful and catastrophic when things are not the way one would very much like them to be"; and Irrational Idea No. 5—"the idea that human unhappiness is externally caused and that people have little or no ability to control their sorrows and disturbances."

Let us now follow several clients briefly as we attempt to deal with their anger.

A Broken Promise: Mr. and Mrs. Teton

Mr. and Mrs. Teton planned on returning to her hometown to live after Mrs. Teton had helped her husband through pharmacy school. Her parents still lived in the small town Mrs. Teton was raised in and they were eager for the day when their daughter and son-in-law would join them again. Mr. Teton was also raised in a small rural town and had every intention of returning to this kind of life after he finished his schooling. After the couple had spent a number of years in the larger city, Mr. Teton received an attractive offer of employment in a Western state. This caught his interest and aroused his budding ambitions. He realized finally that a return to the slow pace and poorer financial future in his wife's town was simply very undesirable. From the day he tried to persuade her of his intentions, their marriage had been repeatedly shaken with quarrels, estrangement, and an overall breakdown of a loving relationship.

She did not become fully resentful of him until it was plain that he really meant to settle in the West—when he accepted an offer without consulting her. The hurt she experienced over his breaking his promise was so strong that she went first from tears to a mild depression, and finally into biting sarcasm. This was soon accompanied by throbbing migraine headaches for which she sought medical help. Her doctor advised counseling along with medication. She accepted only the latter. As their hostility continued, Mr. Teton sought escape in occasional drinking sprees. He and she refused sexual relations with each other as well. When this continued for some weeks and was threatening his studies, both sought help from their minister. Their animosity was so unyielding that he felt unequal to the task and referred them to me.

Mrs. Teton jumped at the chance to make the first complaint and berated her husband for not keeping his word. Feeling that the wife's behavior was the more severe reaction, I decided to try to calm her first. After gaining some background information, I said, "Mrs. Teton, if your husband decides to take the job out West regardless of how you feel, will you go with him or will you leave him?"

"Oh, I'd go with him, of course. I love Bill even though I'm very angry with him. But I wouldn't like it and I'm afraid I'd be mad at him for a long time for breaking his promise."

"Then wouldn't you be better off going with him and *not* being angry?"

"Go cheerfully? How am I supposed to do that? I'm not a saint."

"You don't have to be a saint. Just accept it and make the most of it."

"I've tried that but it won't work. Sure, I can do that with other things he's done which have irritated me. But this, well I just can't believe he'd be so selfish as to insist on doing something that he knows displeases me so much and is a real breach of trust. As though that weren't bad enough, he did it behind my back, besides. I've worked hard helping Bill through school, believing all the time we'd settle down back home near my folks. That's really what makes me mad."

"Not really, Mrs. Teton," I corrected her. "Your husband's decision to go West is not what angers you at all. It's what you're telling yourself because he broke his promise."

"You bet it is, Dr. Hauck. Every time I just think of how unfair this is I get a headache."

It would appear that the client understands the true source of her misery. She does not. To her it is still her husband who made her angry. The counselor should not be misled by such statements of agreement this early in counseling. This is a misunderstanding and must be clarified. Only after rational principles have been explained to the client can we have any assurance that both parties are talking about the same thing.

"I'm sure you do, Mrs. Teton, but try to understand the point I'm making. It's you who are giving yourself these headaches, not your husband. He doesn't make you mad, you do."

"Yes, I know. But if he wouldn't insist on moving West, I wouldn't feel the way I do."

"True enough, but even though he is going West he isn't angering you. Rather, it's what you're telling yourself about his decision to move that's bothering you. The things you think give you a headache and make you angry."

"The things I think make me angry?"

"Yes, what do you tell yourself just before you get angry?"

"That Bill is mean and unfair to go back on his promise," was her quick reply.

"That's not quite all you're thinking, Mrs. Teton. That idea is quite sensible because Bill *is* unfair for going back on his word."

"So why shouldn't I get mad if he's unfair?"

"Because he has a right to be mean and unfair."

"He does? Who said so?"

"It's simply part of his God-given nature. He's a mortal, fallible human with all the strengths and weaknesses all mortals have, including that of changing his mind. Since he's imperfect to begin with, it makes sense to realize he should break his word."

"Why should he make a promise in the first place and then think it's okay to go back on it?"

"Why shouldn't he? That's a perfectly normal, human act. Not being God himself, he behaves like a human and does the rotten things humans are supposed to do, such as break promises. You're sore at your husband because he refuses to behave faultlessly as you define it."

"No, I'm not. We made the agreement together and now he's reneging on it just to suit himself."

"Right. Now, why shouldn't he?"

"Because it's not right, that's why."

"Granted. Now tell me why he shouldn't do anything wrong?"

"I'm supposed to approve of his wrongdoings?"

"Not approve of his wrongdoings, but at least approve of him. Your trouble is that you seriously believe Bill is wicked for doing what he did and should be treated badly and with contempt because he has behaved badly."

I have stated Irrational Idea No. 3 (people are bad and should be severely blamed for their faults), in the hope that she can begin to learn the basic reason for her disturbance. It is apparent that she is ambivalent toward him, loving and hating almost simultaneously. Unless she can agree that (*a*) she has this belief, and (*b*) it is irrational, we will get nowhere. All further discussion with her must keep these goals in sight. Nothing short of their attainment will permit her to forgive him and will bring her peace of mind.

She responded: "Right, he's terrible for doing this behind my back and he should be taught a real good lesson. If I were a man, I'd beat him to a pulp."

"Don't you believe what the Bible says about not being overcome by evil but returning good for evil?"

"Sure I do. I'd like to turn the other cheek and I often do. But I just can't about this."

"Sure you can. You mean you won't. And the reason you won't forgive him is that you mistakenly believe people are bad and wicked when they behave poorly and that hating them is the best way to get them to change."

"I suppose that's correct. However, even if it's wrong to hate him I don't think I can get myself to overlook it. I simply can't forget what he's done."

"I'm not suggesting you do forget what he's done. All

I'm asking is whether you have to blame him for his action and if you must treat him so unforgivingly. The damage is done. The job has been agreed upon. All you can realistically do at this time is go along with it calmly and make the most of it."

"But how do I do that? And furthermore, why *should* I go along with it?"

"Let me answer your second question first. You ought to go along with it because it seems he's determined to settle in the West, whether he has a good reason or not. If your marriage is worth saving, you have no choice but to follow him, or else there won't be a marriage. It would obviously dissolve if he took off and you stayed behind, don't you think?"

"Yes, I'm sure you're right."

"Then, if you want a marriage and the only way you can keep it is to go with him, it follows you should go along. It's that simple. Now, about your first question, how to do it calmly. That's easily done, too, if you will work on changing your belief that he deserves a hard time because of it. If you would put yourself in his place for a while, you might see why he is so insistent on moving his family away from relatives. Maybe he's afraid of too much interference, or afraid that a job in a small town will bore him to death or not satisfy any of his ambitions."

"He's used all those arguments already, but I can't buy them. My folks are not busybodies, and he doesn't have to make a million to make me happy."

"All in-laws interfere somewhat, and besides, maybe a million would make *him* happy. Isn't that legitimate?"

"Not when he's just thinking of himself."

"You mean he's selfish when he thinks of himself but just and fair when he thinks of you?"

"No, he's just and fair when he does what he promises to do."

"Even if he now thinks it would be wrong to do so? For example, if you promised your friend you'd go on a hike with her next Wednesday, would you still go if it rained heavily that day?"

"That's different. After all, it's understood that we'd go on a hike only if the weather permitted."

"Right. There are a whole set of unspoken assumptions whenever a promise is made. And it's the same with respect to your husband's promise to settle in your hometown. In that case it was assumed that his love for small towns would remain unchanged, that his ambitions would not rise, and lastly, that he would not continue to mind the sort of interference he'd get by living near in-laws. None of these feelings are the same today. Therefore, it makes as much sense for him to go through with his original plans as it would for you to go hiking in a downpour next Wednesday merely because you said you would go on a hike that day."

"I think I'm beginning to see your point," she finally conceded, "but I confess it doesn't do much for my resentment. I still find it hard to forgive him."

"That's only because you sincerely believe that *people* are bad when they *behave* badly and that they must be soundly criticized for behaving imperfectly. Unless you seriously question that false idea, you'll always find yourself upset when people act badly. You've got to learn to expect wrong behavior from others, not because they're bad, but because they're human and fallible. What you should have told yourself when your husband changed his mind was: 'I don't like what Bill did. He's wrong for handling this thing the way he did, but after all he's human. He has a right to be wrong. No need to dislike him merely because he's frustrating me. I'll still try, however, to get him to change his mind. But I'll do it calmly and sweetly. He may give in at that approach. If I get angry and blaming, he's likely to get angry also and resist my plans all the more.' Now, Mrs. Teton, if you can learn to control your bitterness by using this reasoning, you may get your way more often, but whether you get your way or not, at least you won't be upset."

She quickly saw the advantage in this last suggestion. "I must say I agree with what you just said. I'm beginning to see that being upset over a frustration can be worse than the frustration in the first place."

"Excellent, Mrs. Teton. And you can avoid this anytime in the future if you'll only accept humans as humans and stop demanding perfect behavior from them. Or if you'd care to remember your Sunday school days, recall that very sound lesson from Matthew: "Judge not, that ye be not judged. For with what judgment ye judge, ye shall be judged; and with what measure ye mete, it shall be measured to you again" (Matt. 7:1-2).

"How true that is, doctor. I've known all along that Bill was treating me worse as I became more blaming, only I didn't know how to stop it."

"Well, you can stop it quickly if you'll stop the blaming. You may still find yourself moving West, but you'll do it calmly if you stop believing he is terrible and ought to be berated. It's easier said than done, incidentally, because your old habit of blaming others is still very strong. But if you earnestly challenge that silly belief, you'll definitely overcome this problem in time. Simply convince yourself that people *will* commit errors and they *can't* avoid them at times, that it's part of their nature to be imperfect, and that they *should* behave wrongly many times in their lives. That will calm you. Then, after you've gained your self-control, try to get your own way by nicer methods. And if that doesn't work, accept things as they are."

Mr. Teton and his wife continued in counseling for two months more, during which time their irrational ideas were questioned so persistently that they both began to alter them. By the time Mr. Teton's final exams approached, he and his wife were getting along so well that he passed them handsomely. They agreed to try it in the West for a year and if for any reason he or she were still unhappy after that period, they agreed to return to her hometown as originally planned.

An Inconsiderate Family: Mrs. Charter

In the case of the Tetons, it was Irrational Idea No. 3 that received the focus of our attention. Actually, we could have discussed Irrational Ideas 4 and 5 along with Idea No. 3, but for purposes of demonstration we avoided doing this. Anger is usually a combination of three ideas rather than one, although one may appear to dominate the other two. In the case of Mrs. Charter, the main sources of her intense emotional upheaval were Irrational Idea No. 4—"that it is awful and catastrophic when things are not the way one would very much like them to be," and Irrational Idea No. 5—"that human unhappiness is externally caused and that people have little or no ability to control their sorrows and disturbances."

Mrs. Charter was fairly calm the first time I met her.

However, she quickly related her problem—the inability to control her violent anger, which repeatedly flared up at the slightest injustice. When frustrated for days at a time, she would invariably have to be taken to the local hospital and there be sedated for several days until calmed. Her husband was eager to do what he could to please her, but he had found over the years that her demands knew no bounds. Eventually he became less concerned with her complaints. Mrs. Charter became more incensed at this indifference, to the point where her hostility frightened her four children and alienated her from her neighbors. After repeated suggestions from her family doctor to seek counseling, she finally agreed only when he threatened not to see her again.

Her list of complaints was endless. Her husband made no effort to keep the house clean; her children were noisy; the neighbors were busybodies. She found fault wherever she looked.

"If only," she added, "I could get my husband to discipline the kids at times, what a blessing that would be. But no, he just sits in front of the TV set and lets them wreck the place. Small wonder I get upset."

Her further remarks gave every indication that she was a sincere person, trying hard to do her best to be a good friend, housekeeper, mother, and wife. It was also apparent that when her sincere efforts and hard work were not quickly and completely rewarded, she took this as an unbearable act of injustice that justified any degree of frankness, including the most blunt tongue-lashing. When she felt in the right she was totally unforgiving of another's errors and experienced the keenest sense of righteous anger. It was obvious that she believed her unhappy state was caused by others and that it was positively dreadful not to be treated fairly by others when she had first done nothing but good for them.

To this last observation she said: "Of course I'm mad when others ignore what I've done for them. My husband wants his meals on time and his shirts ironed, and the kids want me to do all sorts of things for them. But when *I* want some consideration they fight me all the way."

She has stated that she *wants* their cooperation. From the fact that she gets angry we know this is only half the truth. She must be shown that she is constantly *demanding* all that she desires.

"You'd be completely unruffled, Mrs. Charter, if you really believed that you only wanted different behavior from your family. Granted, that's the first thought that goes through your mind when you judge them. But the thought you have immediately after that one is of a different nature, and it's *that* thought, rather than your family, which is creating all this resentment and bitterness."

"What thought is that?"

"That they *should* be considerate and appreciative of all your efforts simply because you would like them to be so. That doesn't make good sense."

"What's wrong with wanting them to help me out and mind me once in a while?"

"Mrs. Charter, it isn't what you *want* that does the damage, it's what you *demand* that causes all this trouble. You wrongly insist that because your requests are reasonable ones your family *must* be just and fair and grant them to you."

"So what's so unfair about that?" she replied with a touch of indignation.

"Plenty. You have no legitimate right to demand anything from anyone. Why, for instance, must your husband be considerate of you, merely because you would like him to be? Who says he can't be unfair and inconsiderate if he chooses to be?"

"He can be as selfish as he likes with anyone else for all I care, but not with me, not if I haven't given him reason to be."

"There you go again, insisting that he must appreciate what you do for him, because you'd like him to be appreciative. Suppose I told you I'd prefer to see you in a red dress rather than a blue one. Would I have any legitimate right to demand that you wear red from now on?"

"Of course not, Dr. Hauck. But surely that isn't quite the same thing. I'm talking about fair and just behavior, not fashions."

"Fine, I'll use your example then. If I don't think you are fair in the way you get angry at your family, do I have the legitimate right to command you to stop treating them as you do? I'm sure you'd agree that I don't have that right. And yet, I'd be doing the same thing you are. I would want something and then convert it into a need and insist I had to have my own way. Your wishes are perfectly sensible and harmless. And I suspect your family life would be much better for you and the others if they would take more pains to keep an orderly house and help each other more. That's not a reason, however, why they must be sweet and cooperative. It's only your false belief that it's terrible and dreadful not to have things your own way that makes you angry when that demand is frustrated. Had you kept these sensible wishes at the level of wishes and your family did not go along with you, your reaction could not be any more than regret or disappointment. It isn't until after you mentally make a demand out of that wish that you must be pleased, that they *should* behave like angels, that they *cannot* be selfish, that you become disturbed if they don't give you your way. Can't you see how dictatorial you're being? You're saying no one has any rights but you!"

"Are you suggesting they're right by not caring more about what goes on at home?"

"No, not at all. If they're as you say, I'd agree they're all inconsiderate and are treating your efforts shabbily. What I do mean is that even though they're wrong, they aren't terrible people for being wrong. They're just weak, inconsiderate people, who perhaps don't know how to act differently and, therefore, have a right to be wrong."

"Then should I just sit back and let them fight and scream and make a mess of the place?" was her expected reply.

"By no means, Mrs. Charter. Do all you can to train them along lines you see fit. Only do it calmly. Don't upset yourself when they do wrong by believing neurotically that they shouldn't make mistakes. That's foolish and will only end up by giving you high blood pressure. Then you'll have to deal with the frustration that they gave you, *and* the painful emotions that you gave yourself by foolishly believing that others can upset you and that it's awful when you don't get your way. Instead, tell yourself that they're behaving badly, that they have a right to, and that you don't approve of it but will attempt to change them calmly and without malice. That way you stand a better chance of getting them to change, and you won't be making mincemeat of yourself at the same time."

"You mean I should actually be sweet and loving when they're impossible?"

"Of course, why not? After all, they're not upsetting you

in the first place, you are. Secondly, you'll get their co-operation more easily if you stop yelling at them and gently show or persuade them to do what you want. You get more flies with honey than vinegar, you know."

"You're so right, and I wish I could be that way. I've seen many times how rattled and scared my kids get after I scream at them. They're so upset they blunder again a minute later. Just the other day my daughter, Linda, broke a dish while washing and I scolded her so badly she promptly broke another one. I got so mad I flopped myself on my bed and cried."

"And all because you told yourself that Linda must never break a dish?"

"Well, should she?" she asked.

"Naturally she should. How in the world is it possible to wash dishes day in and day out and never break one? Haven't you ever broken a dish?"

"Sure I have, but not like my kids do. They're awful."

"Then sweetly show them what they're doing wrong so they can learn to do better. Convince yourself that you don't need perfect dishwashers although that would be very desirable, and if you then calmly teach them what's wrong, they'll eventually improve. That way you'll have spared yourself an ulcer and done something constructive about the problem itself—a vast improvement, I'd say."

Attention to the pain of an actual but trivial event in the client's life is most worthwhile. It has a sense of immediacy and relevancy for him not duplicated by a discussion of theory. Theory must not be ignored, however. Unless it can also demonstrate the *general* case through the use of common occurrences, the sensibleness of the theory makes progress unlikely.

"All that you've said makes a great deal of sense, I must admit. I still don't see that I'm totally at fault for what happens at home though. I gather I'm supposed to go home, not make any demands, not let anyone disturb me, and hope they shape up because I've become a sweet and loving person. I'm not sure that's going to work."

"I agree. That's not going to work because that's not what I said."

If the client does not at some time make summary statements to permit the counselor to assess the degree of comprehension, he should make every effort during the session to ask her to repeat the salient features of what he has been attempting to teach. This feedback is essential for determining the areas of misunderstanding.

I continued: "I've been dealing primarily with only one of your problems, your anger. What you do about your family and friends after you've calmed yourself down is the second problem. Nowhere have I suggested that you ignore your kids and permit them to become wild Indians merely because you aren't furious with them. I focused on the anger first, because the solution to their behavior cannot be faced until you change and control yourself."

"So I'm not supposed to remain indifferent about these things, just calm and unresentful, and then teach them or discipline them if I have to. But I mustn't feel this devil inside of me, is that it?"

"Right. And you'll be surprised at how much better you are at getting your way and how much better behaved they will be when you're more loving."

"I'll give it a try. Hope it works," she concluded.

Her second session started out with: "I'm amazed at how right you were. I did just what you said and I felt just wonderful. All week long I've been telling myself my husband and kids can't upset me and whatever I want from them is okay but not so important that I have to wind up in the hospital bed for it. Anytime anything went wrong I drilled that into my head and I could just feel the anger melt away. Then I'd discuss my gripes very sweetly with John or the kids and it was amazing how nicely they responded. A couple of times John irritated me with his permissiveness and I was all set to scream at him for not getting our youngest boy to bed while I was making the next day's lunch sandwiches in the kitchen. But I told myself: 'Now wait a minute, girl. John isn't going to hop to if I bite off his ear. So I'd better ask him again sweetly. And anyway, I'm not some kind of a baby who always has to have her way. So he does not act like the responsible father. Who am I to insist that he must be father of the year? So calm down and see what you can do about this irritation instead of working yourself into a jumble of nerves.' It was just wonderful, just wonderful. I never had such a week in my life."

Such dramatic changes are by no means commonplace for RET. Nor are they rare. They occurred in this instance because the client's motivation was high and, in addition to the few excerpts described above, the actual hour was a good deal more forceful and detailed. Some clients can grasp RET principles amazingly quickly, irrespective (within limits) of their intelligence. This case was presented to show that such swift changes are possible through the appeal to reason.

Rational-emotive psychotherapy is so akin to instruction that I have often found myself wishing for a blackboard on which to diagram my remarks. A sheet of paper has served just as well to make my thoughts crystal clear.

I have not hesitated to use this means to describe these concepts. It is particularly easy to illustrate diagrammatically the mechanics of anger that relate to Irrational Idea No. 4—"the idea that it is awful and catastrophic when things are not the way one would very much like them to be."

ATTITUDES

Healthy (Avoiding anger)	Unhealthy (Leading to anger)
A goal expressed as	*A goal expressed as*
A wish	A need
A desire	A demand
A preference	A necessity
and requested thus:	*and requested thus:*
I wish you would	You should
I want you to	You ought to
I prefer that you	You must
—if frustrated, leads to	*—if frustrated, leads to*
Regret	Resentment
Disappointment	Bitterness
	Anger
	Hatred

The client can be encouraged to keep the slip of paper and review it as the need arises. Some of my clients have with profit kept it in their wallets or tacked it up at home for ready reference and easy reminder. The creative counselor can make similar diagrams of other important concepts. Even if he jots down the sort of healthy thoughts he wants his client to remember and instructs him to review them when he is becoming upset, he may be quite surprised by the frequent use to which these notes will be put. The counselor must never forget that he is not always essential to the process of attitudinal change in counseling. Books, notes, diagrams, and tapes—all instructional techniques—have as much validity in RET as they have in the classroom.

7
Undermining the Loved Ones

THE MINISTER IS OFTEN, BY HIS UPBRINGING, A KIND, ACCEPTing, and uncritical person. He prefers to see the good in people and is reluctant to attack the respected figures in a person's life, especially the members of a client's family. In society this is unquestionably a sign of refinement and good breeding. In counseling it is hypocrisy and easily leads to failure.

Each client comes to us with strong beliefs, parentally nurtured, which he uncritically assumes to be true. Many are, in point of fact, seriously false. These are the final and direct causes of the victim's needless mental torment. Unless his faith in these neurotic beliefs can be shaken, the neurotic is doomed to further emotional distress.

Faith in an idea is often, more accurately, loyalty to a person. For this reason, excessive loyalty must be weakened. Without committing a disservice to the sincere parents of our client, or causing him to disrespect his spouse. we must, for his and their sakes, undermine the hold they have over his attitudes. Should the pastor assume such an onerous chore? He must, if he intends to be of service.

The client is trained from childhood to honor and obey his mother and father. As he matures, the normal adult develops a set of values which may or may not coincide with those of his parents. He does this, guilt-free in the secure knowledge that each has a right to his opinion and that dishonor is not implied by disagreement. As an adult he will no longer obey mechanically, yet will continue to respect his elders.

The neurotic adult will have been taught that it is sinful and dishonorable to disobey his elders. Disagreement is equated with disrespect. He fails, therefore, to think for himself and instead regards his fallible parents as saints.

This is a perceptual distortion of their merits and does these authorities a genuine disservice. They are mere mortals. In his heart, however, the client does not truly believe this. His childish awe for their superior wisdom and experience seriously distorts present reality. This reality must be made abundantly clear to the submissive adult and his faith in their constant rightness must be shaken.

To do this the minister may have to be harsh in his denouncement of this authority figure, be he parent, spouse, employer, or anyone else, and still avoid any danger that he will undermine the client's love or respect for these persons. This is a delicate maneuver but a vital one. Without it, the false gods created by the subject's impressionable mind will continue to dominate his life. Without it, he will continue to honor them out of fear and hypocrisy but forever fall short of their respect, which is the purpose of the sacrifice.

The following is typical: Mr. Thomas, age forty, had had an intermittently smooth relationship with his wife over the years. The only serious menace to their marriage was his demanding father. So persistent were this man's demands on his son that the latter often ignored his own work and family to placate his irate father. For years Mrs. Thomas had put up with playing second fiddle. Finally she rebelled. Mr. Thomas found himself uncomfortably in the middle, between two furious people, one accusing him of disrespect, the other of indifference. Unable to defy his father and to please his wife, he entered into numerous quarrels with her and ended by numbing his guilt with alcohol. Thus, insult was added to injury, and on the verge of divorce, she came to me for professional help.

Though I might have helped her to accept Mr. Thomas' weakness, I regarded this as an inferior solution and preferred instead to help the husband directly. Fortunately, he agreed to see me.

Father and son had similar businesses—clothing establishments—several miles apart. When ill or on vacation, Mr. Thomas, Sr., would impose upon his son to check the cash each night and close up his store. In addition, he frequently called upon his son to pick up goods for him and to perform numerous other odd chores that could as easily have been hired out to others. To save himself money, the older man never hesitated to use the free services of his son.

It was apparent from our initial discussion that my client had two irrational beliefs that permitted this situation: (1) that he needed his father's approval, and (2) that he had to blame himself when he was not a perfect son or an ideal husband. As the first idea created reasons for the second, it was regarded as more basic and it required our immediate attention. To help the son accomplish a mature perception of his father, however, it would be necessary to topple the patriarch from the lofty pedestal on which his son had placed him. Only then could the son stand up to his father and feel comfortable when not giving his complete approval.

"Apparently, Mr. Thomas, you feel your father is often making unreasonable demands of you. Why do you obey them if they're foolish?" I asked.

"Because he's done so much for me—even set me up in business. I can hardly refuse him now, can I?"

"Of course you can—and should," I retorted. "If you don't, he'll have you jumping through hoops."

"He practically does that now," he laughed. "Still, I can't bring myself to refuse him anything."

"That's nonsense and you know it. Let me show you how you don't really believe that yourself. Suppose your father told you to jump into the lake. Or suppose he commanded you to sell your business or do something else equally ridiculous. Would you do it?"

"He'd never ask me to do anything like that."

"Wouldn't he? What do you call what he's doing right now? Here he is, perfectly able to hire help and he insists on you giving him a hand every time it's going to cost him normal wages."

"But those are just favors a son is expected to do."

"Even at the cost of your own family harmony? Your father knows full well how your wife disapproves of his taking your time for his affairs, but he doesn't consider her feelings for one minute, does he? I'd say your dad was an unreasonable tyrant to take advantage of his relationship with you. He doesn't need your help for an instant, yet he pesters you for assistance constantly and doesn't give a hoot how his demands inconvenience you. If you ask me, the whole thing ought to work in reverse. He's the one with all the money. If anyone needs a helping hand from time to time, it's you."

He did not like the attack on his father and quickly sprang to his defense. "I don't want you to think my father is all bad. Over the years he's been swell to me."

"Oh, don't get me wrong either, Mr. Thomas," I answered. "I'm sure your father is a fine man and that you love him a great deal. All I'm trying to point out is that he's not perfect and that he happens to have some unfortunate habits, such as being overly demanding."

"There you go, tearing him down again."

"I'm not criticizing him, only his neurotic habits. Let's be realistic about this. Your father, with all his wonderful qualities, is nevertheless bossy and egocentric."

"And you can still say he's probably a wonderful guy?"

"Of course, because that's absolutely true too isn't it?"

"Yes, I suppose he isn't perfect, is he? Have I been treating him as though he were?"

"That's the way it seems to me. You know intellectually that he can be plenty foolish, but when the time comes for you to treat him as you'd treat any other foolish person, you suddenly do a complete about-face and convince yourself he's in the right after all."

"That's for sure. I'd never take his kind of treatment from anyone else," Mr. Thomas assured me.

"And what happens when you stand up to others?"

"Nothing. They take it and respect me for my conviction."

"Does your father respect you?"

"Not really, not as I want him to respect me. Nothing I do seems to earn that."

"If you were my son, I think I'd lose respect for you too," I affirmed.

"But why?"

"Because you don't respect yourself. You'd let me use

you like a doormat. How much respect could I have for a doormat?"

"None, of course. Why doesn't my father see this about me and encourage me to stand up to him?"

"There you go again, making an all-knowing, godlike man out of a self-centered neurotic. He doesn't think he's doing anything wrong. He honestly believes he's entitled to your undying obedience. Is this perfection?"

My client remarked that perhaps he had a childish view of his father's omniscience, but that even this was little consolation in getting him to defy the older man.

I resumed: "Mr. Thomas, you not only have the right to deny your father in many of his demands, but the obligation. Can't you see what your kindness has done to this man over the past twenty-five years?"

"What my *kindness* has done?"

"Yes, your willingness to jump whenever he snaps his fingers. You've helped make him an eighty-year-old spoiled brat. He's got it in his head that he's entitled to everything he asks for and if he doesn't get his way he has to blow his stack."

"I've always given in to him so he wouldn't blow his stack."

"I know you did. How successful was that technique?"

"Not very, I'm afraid. I've gone out of my way to please him and it seems he wants to boss me all the more. My brother, now—Dad respects him. But do you think Bob ever did anything for his father like I've done? No, sir! They used to fight like cats and dogs, and he's the one Dad keeps throwing up to me now. I get no appreciation for what I've done. How do you figure that out?"

"Because he's immature, neurotic. How else can you explain why a father likes the indifferent child and abuses the kind one? He has the philosophy that you are a fool if others take advantage of you. He could not get his other son to kowtow to him, so he respects him just like he respects himself for not letting others dominate him. You, by allowing yourself to be dominated, go to the bottom of the totem pole. That's stupid and unchristian thinking, but that's your dear old dad for you."

His next remark suggested that Mr. Thomas was contemplating self-assertion and saw an obvious consequence that he had always felt he must avoid.

"If I do what you're suggesting, I'm afraid it'll be quits between him and me."

"It probably will be, at least for a time. Would that bother you very much?"

"Yes, it would."

"Then don't make so much out of his disapproval. I can see how you would have been vitally concerned over his love when you were a youngster. However, you're an adult now. You don't mean to tell me you still need his approval, do you?"

We need not follow Mr. Thomas into this area. Our purpose was to bring him to the realization that father was not the Almighty and could be faced as readily as any other mortal. By giving him a realistic picture of his father we have partially taken away the client's notion that he *must* not disobey him. This can now be followed up with instructions in *how* to defy the father, how he defeats those ends, and what steps the client will have to follow to avoid giving in most of the time.

At first, of course, Mr. Thomas only gave his father excuses why he could not satisfy each of his demands. As his total faith in Dad's rightness was challenged weekly, he eventually began to see the older man's basic selfishness for what it was and that he, Mr. Thomas, Jr., had every right not to give in repeatedly. This permitted him to exercise firmness without guilt; to feel self-confidence without forcing his will over others; and to appreciate his father's merits realistically, while seeing his faults.

In one of our last sessions he had this to say: "A strange thing happened to my father and me. We're finally getting along better than we ever have. After our last fight he finally saw the light. He realized that his days of making a monkey out of me were over, and he began to look up to me for the first time that I can remember. Would you believe it, he *asks* me if I'd care to do this or that for him instead of ordering me, and unless it's very important he won't bother me about his business affairs at all. Why, only last week he came to me for advice. Would you believe it?" he asked laughingly.

Contrary to common belief, divesting the client of unrealistic attitudes about significant figures frees him from childhood passivity and releases his own mature judgment. Unless this is first done for the client by actively undermining his worshipful attitudes toward such figures, he usually cannot initiate the process, so intense would be the guilt. Regardless of who these figures are who receive this *neurotic* respect, they must be dethroned. They are not denounced as bad or worthless people, but rather as fallible, ignorant, or neurotic people merely doing their best.

My approach with another client, a young man who was poorly raised by a well-meaning set of relatives, illustrates this point.

Stanley, eighteen years old, had recently been spending money wildly, made exaggerated claims about having hidden wealth, and boasted about his great power to command others. This was a brief but first attack of grandiose utterances, and, after he had been treated with tranquilizers at the local hospital, he was referred to me.

It was quite obvious that underneath these grandiose ravings lay strong feelings of inferiority. As we talked, it appeared that he had been ill-treated and rejected by his relatives for minor infractions of household rules.

"They'd scold me, send me outside all day, make me go to my room when company came—that sort of thing," he said. "I suppose I had it coming to me."

"I seriously doubt that," I replied as I started to undermine his respect for his surrogate parents. "You were only a kid, doing the sort of things all kids do. I don't think they treated you wisely or fairly at all. Did they treat their own children like this?"

"No, never that I can remember. I always explained that by the fact that they were their natural children and I wasn't."

"Yes, you're probably right. They probably did let that fact make a big difference. Isn't it a shame that they weren't more mature—that they let that fact make them behave so badly?"

"Now wait a minute, doc. I don't want to give you the impression that they weren't wonderful folks. If it hadn't been for them, I would have been raised in an institution."

"I agree with you, Stanley. They did a wonderful thing by taking you into their home. I'm only pointing out that they were limited in their ability to love you and to be objective about a strange boy. As a result they turned out to be a couple of pretty lousy parents, despite their best efforts to do their best."

"You're making it sound like they were responsible for this mess I got myself into. I can't blame them for what happened."

"And you shouldn't blame yourself, Stanley. You're responsible for making exaggerated claims, but the reasons why you thought you needed to make them must be traced back to your foster parents. Had they treated you in a more humane way, you wouldn't have felt impelled to play the big shot. You've been fighting feelings of inferiority for some time now. Where did they come from—the cereal you eat? Obviously not. You feel worthless because they treated you as though you were inferior and worthless. Maybe they were embarrassed, having an orphaned kid in the family. Maybe something else. I don't know and it doesn't matter. The important thing is that *they* had a problem and therefore couldn't do a good job in raising you."

"In other words, I was treated a certain way, not because of anything being wrong with me, but because of what was wrong with them?"

"Weren't you? Do you honestly believe that every set of parents would have handled you the same way? That would have been impossible. You can see that, can't you? Then how can we account for the difference? Since you would have been the same child, the explanation for any difference in your upbringing would rest with the particular parents doing the raising."

"I see what you mean now. I often wondered how it would have been to be the son of the folks down the street. They were wonderful people and they treated me real swell."

"There you go. That's my point. The way you were treated was their responsibility, not yours. Had your foster parents been better educated or more mature, they would have treated you differently. Their shortcomings, not yours, needed correction."

"Gee, I feel real good when you say that, especially that I don't have to hate them for what they did. I know they tried their best even though it was pretty awful at times. But as you say, they weren't perfect. And I don't have to hate myself either just because they treated me like a hateful thing at times. That's their problem, isn't it?"

"Right. Stop thinking of them as superhumans who could do no wrong and you'll like them more and you won't blame yourself for not being the perfect angel they neurotically demanded."

Stanley made a remarkable recovery. In the short space of three consultations he relinquished his hateful notions about himself and even ventured back to visit his relatives. He soon noted how relaxed he was in their presence and how he and they could talk as equals for the first time.

For the clergyman, one of the most difficult teachings to undermine will be the sexual beliefs that the client has absorbed from his parents. This poses the double threat of removing the parent from an honored position of authority while also exposing the minister to a confrontation with his own dogmatic sexual notions. In all likelihood he will meet head on in his client many of his own attitudes. This can be experienced as an unnerving encounter or a magnificent opportunity for growth.

The sexual notions that many children are raised to accept are so neurotic that considerable marital frustration results. These are often the direct teachings, not of the church or its gospel, but of the misguided parents, who have propagandized their belief in the sinfulness of sex. Victims of this upbringing must learn to regard the sex act as a healthy, pleasurable union between man and woman if they are ever to overcome their guilt and inhibition.

To accomplish this end it will first be necessary to undermine the authority (as *experts* on sex) of the parents who taught these beliefs. The pastor will not want to, nor should he, undermine their influence any more than is necessary to accomplish his goals. No one is all wise or all foolish. In deference to all the fine efforts that parents, guardians, or teachers make, we must be discriminating in how critical we become, lest we cast serious doubt over *all* their teachings.

Mrs. Call, age thirty-five, was a happily married woman with three children. She simply could not relax during intercourse, felt shy in disrobing before her husband, and felt guilt whenever the sex act was the least bit pleasurable. As a result, she had never had a climax. In addition to experiencing increasing frustration over the years, she was now beginning to consider herself a failure as a woman. The inevitable depressive moods that followed led her to seek professional help.

She was first shown how her self-blaming thoughts were causing the depression and how her focusing on the evil of sex was so distracting that the enjoyment of sex was impossible. She challenged my beliefs about sex being fun and perfectly moral and this led to a discussion of where she had obtained this sick idea. Her mother, it turned out, had been her prominent instructress. With this determined, it became apparent that the client's respect for her mother as an *authority on sex* would have to be demolished before she could regard the subject in a normal light.

"Tell me, Mrs. Call, what kind of sex life did your mother have?" I asked.

"From all the things she told me I'd have to assume she didn't like it."

neurotic on the subject of sex, and yes, she has the company of millions of other misguided souls who have foolishly turned one of life's greatest pleasures into a nightmare."

"But if it's so common, does it make sense to call it a neurosis?" she inquired.

"Is a cold not a cold if a million people have one?"

"You mean to say, then, back in the days of grandmother, when practically every man and woman felt sex to be at least a little evil, that they were *all* neurotic?"

"About sex—and if they felt pained, of course. What do numbers have to do with it? Wasn't every person during the Middle Ages neurotic on the subject of witches, evil spirits, and other such pain-inducing nonsense?"

"I suppose so. It's just that I thought one wasn't sick if he or she shared the beliefs of the majority, that one was following the accepted customs and beliefs of the times," was her astute retort. "So everyone in Columbus' day who believed the world was flat was also neurotic?"

"Not neurotic, just mistaken. Neurotic thinking has two characteristics: it is false in the first instance, and it causes an internalized pain or a harmful and goal-defeating way of life in the second instance. People were not emotionally upset by their belief that the world was flat. They were simply wrong. Columbus challenged the earth-is-flat hypothesis and disproved it. Without any proof your mother accepted the notion that sex is bad, so it never became pleasurable. Yet, she never let herself think for a moment that it might not be bad, in which case she could have experienced its pleasures in short order."

"And this is what I've done, isn't it? If I question the idea that sex for fun is evil, I'll be able to enjoy it?"

"Definitely. The only thing that makes you inhibited is the idea that it's wrong. Prove to yourself that this idea is silly, and you'll soon find all kinds of new pleasure in your sex life."

Mrs. Call was thoughtful for a moment, but finally said, "I don't know if I can."

"Of course you can! Don't tell me an intelligent person like you actually believes everything else her mother has taught her?"

"No, come to think of it. I smoke and enjoy an occasional drink. Mother strongly disapproves of both."

"Well then, why are you telling me you could successfully challenge and overthrow her ideas on smoking and drinking, but you can't question her ideas about sex?"

"It does seem inconsistent, doesn't it?"

"Not just *seems,* it *is* inconsistent. Treat her sexual teachings as you have treated some of her other teachings that you disagree with, and your sex life will have to improve. The next time you automatically repeat her sexual ideas to yourself, stop a moment and question them. Ask yourself seriously if you *really* are bad for wanting the light on while making love, or if you *really* are a sinner, as she claims, because you feel like you'd want to move your body to increase the sensations. Don't just blindly accept her ideas anymore. Realize finally that mother was wrong about sex and that there is no reason in the wide world why you must follow her sex teachings another night."

Gratifyingly, the client did just that. In time she responded in a lively, spontaneous fashion to her husband (who was delighted with the change), and she still retained deep love and respect for her mother.

More often than has been recognized, this aspect of counseling has been ignored. Counselors have been too timid about dethroning these demigods, or they have not been *dramatic* and *unequivocal* enough to speak with genuine or sincere conviction. The pastor must make no bones about where he stands. It is an all-or-none task. When he realizes this, he has the force of conviction that spurs the client on to a deep reevaluation of his faulty attitudes.

8
Special Considerations

WE SHALL NOW ATTEMPT TO STUDY SEVERAL PERTINENT areas of counseling that have not yet been given the attention they deserve.

Counseling Those of Other Faiths

Several persistent concerns face the pastor if he chooses to refer a client to a counselor of a different faith, be it a clergyman or a professional psychotherapist.

His first concern will be whether or not the client's faith will be weakened and undermined by this exposure. Let us be realistic on this issue and admit that many therapists have ethical views quite different from orthodox religious positions. Some are militantly antichurch and never hesitate to attack religious beliefs, while others have a total indifference to spiritual values.

A second group of professionals to whom the pastor hesitates to make referrals are those whom he regards as conscientious and ethical, but whose faith differs from the client's. He may have a sincere doubt that the client's problem can be fully understood and modified without also infusing the counselor's own religious principles into the consultations.

The first group he will, of course, avoid. The second group, however, has redeeming features that can easily be assessed if the proper effort is made, and if he will focus on the similarity between faiths rather than the minute theological differences that separate some of them. In addition, it should be realized that many counseling problems involve spiritual matters only tangentially, or not at all. The client who is seeking help to overcome shyness, for instance, can well be counseled by a counselor of any faith. But the woman who feels that she has sinned because of an abortion will surely require a therapist whom the pastor can trust as being in sympathy with her conviction that she has committed a wrong.

The Emotional Side of RET

In the preceding pages the reader has been presented with a rationale for appealing to reason. He will surely have noticed the unique quality of the language the counselor uses to communicate reason to his client. He has by now observed a style of speech used by this counselor that may strike him as unprofessional and blunt. He is correct.

Logic is cold, serious, and humorless. Only the philosopher is forgiven his eccentric attachment to the subject. Yet logic remains the very substance of our peace of mind, whether we be housewife or professor. Logic is indispensable, but its forbidding qualities must be canceled through the use of warm, vigorous, expressive, and emotive language. In this way the black and white bones of reason are given lifelike colors.

It is the rare client who can bring himself to question his value systems purely on the basis of logic. This is especially true for all those millions who are not members of the intelligentsia. A flair for expression is almost necessary to convey certain notions to people in the trades or to people who have a limited educational background. Actually, experience has shown that ideas colored emotively are more quickly grasped even among the better educated. Far from being sterile, RET makes constant use of emotionally charged statements to enhance the experience of the positive affects, such as joy, elation, humor, and desire —while discouraging the use of the harmful affects, such as hatred, fear, and jealousy. At times these statements are shocking, brutally honest, or delightfully humorous— but always very human. If used judiciously and with regard for the client's right to guide his own life, the emotive expressions create friendliness in the client rather than distance. The client quickly learns not to take himself too seriously or to fear that he cannot speak to someone who usually is far beyond him educationally. The quality of speech is too informal to permit this. Rapport is quickly established and, more than in any other technique, personal details of the most surprising nature are related in rapid succession. It is the speech used between friends.

The parallel columns below present common counseling remarks. On the left the counselor's thoughts are expressed in a cold, formal, professional way, while on the right the same thoughts are paraphrased in warm, friendly, emotive language.

As written, some of the remarks on the right seem only harsh and blaming. Fortunately the voice can soften these words. "Your thinking is way off base" can be said sneeringly, pityingly, or humorously. The expressions in the right-hand column can show greater concern for the client's welfare than the corresponding expressions on the left. The truck driver will feel a common bond with his counselor when so addressed.

Cold Expressions	*Warm Expressions*
1. Your behavior is very self-defeating.	1. You're your own worst pain in the neck.
2. Must you mistreat yourself?	2. Why the devil do you have to crucify yourself?
3. You surely were upset!	3. You sure were acting neurotically!
4. Your ideas are inaccurate.	4. Your thinking is way off base.
5. You didn't try very hard.	5. You really goofed off.
6. Would the consequences be serious?	6. Is it gonna kill you?
7. Why do you believe that?	7. Where the devil did you get that idea?
8. You'll have to persevere.	8. You'll have to stick it out.

Naturally, no attempt should be made to employ such language faddishly. It should be used in varying degrees, depending on how forceful the counselor feels he must be to carry his thought. Some clients will require little of it. Others feel distant unless always addressed in down-to-earth terms.

Inertia and Pessimism—Twin Roadblocks

Nothing in counseling is so frustrating to the counselor as is the failure of his client to put into effect the new way of life the counselor is so willing to impart. After the subject has been shown his illogical beliefs, after these beliefs have been connected where necessary to forgotten memories and events, and after the etiology of these beliefs has been described, there is at times a disheartening lack of improvement. If the pastor is reasonably sure that his groundwork has been adequate, but substantial change is not noticed, he must ask himself what other irrational ideas are blocking the way. Experience has shown one or both of the following to be present: Irrational Idea No. 7—"the idea that it is easier to avoid than to face certain life difficulties and self-responsibilities," and Irrational Idea No. 9—"the idea that one's past history is an all-important determiner of one's present behavior and that because something once strongly affected one's life, it should indefinitely have a similar effect."

There is nothing particularly easy about overcoming long-established thinking habits. They are usually well-ingrained behavior patterns, which will attempt to assert themselves each time they seem appropriate. Only the most diligent kind of application, applied each time or, at the very least, much of the time that an irrational idea raises its ugly head, can release the hold that these beliefs have on their host. All too often, unfortunately, while the counselor is instructing and guiding his student in the techniques of emotional control, he fails to detect the presence of this hidden agent that is bringing all his efforts to a halt.

To remove this roadblock, the client is asked again what it is that he is probably telling himself that is making his efforts at change come to naught. He may respond with: "It's so hard, I don't know if I can do it. I know what I'm supposed to do to remain calm, but darned if I can manage to do it." In this case we can suspect immediately that he is evading his responsibility to himself in the belief that he will gain more relief by ignoring the learning task than by facing it. Irrational Idea No. 7 should at once be explained to the client and the reasons should be given why it is irrational.

On the other hand, the client may respond with: "I feel it's so hopeless. I doubt if I'll ever be able to change. I keep wondering if I'm just not made this way." In this case he is suffering from Irrational Idea No. 9 (the notion that a history of having a problem means that it cannot be overcome).

To overcome inertia, I have found the arguments described in the following interview usually successful in creating forward movement again.

Mr. Rodin had such frequent temper flare-ups at work that he feared losing his job. He seemed to be showing no progress whatever after six sessions, so he was asked: "Why do you suppose you aren't making any headway, Mr. Rodin? After all, you seem to understand how you get yourself upset and how you can talk yourself out of it."

"I'm not sure. I only know I still want to set any guy straight who gets in my way."

"We already know how you develop that attitude and what you can do about removing it. I'm wondering why you aren't making yourself stop the anger."

"I guess it's just easier to blow my stack. Trying to talk myself into being calm when someone is bugging me just doesn't seem natural."

"It certainly isn't natural, but neither is brushing your teeth. Would you let your mouth get full of cavities merely because nature is taking its normal course?"

"You're saying it's normal and natural for me to get mad, but that doesn't make it the smart thing to do—is that it?"

"Precisely. It's also normal and natural to get fat, grow old, eat with your fingers, and so on. Yet you try your hardest to diet most of the time, to exercise and get physical checkups to protect your health as long as possible, and to eat with utensils, because it's neater in the long run. These, and hundreds of other unnatural and non-normal things, are done most of the time by everyone, because life is better that way. It's the same with thinking calmly when someone frustrates you. It's normal to want to punch him in the nose and to raise your blood pressure over the insult, but is it good for you? That's what you must continually ask yourself."

"I just don't know if I can. I think about what you've told me after I blow up. Then it's too late."

"What are you telling yourself that convinces you that you can't use those sensible thoughts to help avoid the anger?"

"I don't know."

"I suspect you're telling yourself that it's too much bother to grit your teeth a few minutes while you calmly think over why the person who just belittled you has a right to do so, is really a fine person who's just acting badly for the moment, and deserves a soft smile and warm response from you rather than a fist in the mouth."

Mr. Rodin laughed as he recognized how closely the suggestion touched the truth. "I guess I've been thinking something like that all along. How much simpler it is to cut some wise guy down to size."

"There's the rub, isn't it? Is it really easier to shoot your mouth off, churn your insides to pieces, and endanger your job than it is to face this business of learning how to handle your anger? Granted, you may get immediate relief if you even the score, but how good is that for you in the long run? It seems you have another irrational notion that you've got to straighten out in addition to the one that creates your anger and resentment. That notion goes like this: It is easier to avoid and run away from difficult problems than it is to face them."

Whereas inertia, laziness, and procrastination are related to Irrational Idea No. 7, pessimism is the result of Irrational Idea No. 9—the idea that one's past has a strong and unyielding effect on the present and future. So long as the client leans on this belief, real movement is out of the question. He must be shown that the past has only as much influence over him as he permits it to have. The greatest control of the past comes in fact not from one's history, but from the belief that history makes an unbreakable tie from which there is no escape. If this were true, pessimism would be a sensible response. When this notion has been seriously challenged, even the most long-standing habits have been known to give way.

If Mr. Rodin had suggested that it was impossible for him to change because he had had temper outbursts for thirty years, I would have cited several experiences he himself has had, or might have, that disprove this idea. Is he right-handed? Then would it really be impossible for him to write if he lost his right hand? How is it he managed to learn to drive a car? According to his position this should have been impossible, for how can one learn something if it was unlearned until he was sixteen years old? Is not learning control of anger the same as acquiring any new skill? Practice, analysis of mistakes, and new trials again are all that are practically needed to master new habits. He has succeeded literally hundreds of times already. Why should this issue of learning self-control be any different?

When Pastors Fail as Counselors

Ministers as a group have some characteristics in common which, for purposes of counseling, are wonderfully to their advantage. Other characteristics are distinctly to their disadvantage. It behooves each counselor to be aware of these strong and weak points so that he can utilize the strong ones to the fullest, and correct or avoid the others. Let us first discuss those characteristics of ministers that tend to contribute toward failure in counseling.

1. The clergyman is often a self-blamer and a perfectionist. He, after all, is a product of our sick and irrational society no less than his client is. He was reared with the same neurotic beliefs we were all exposed to. Unless he has recently been exposed to more rational thinking, he will commit what I have called the Error of Neurotic Agreement.[34] This means that instruction in counseling can go no further than the point where full agreement between counselor and client has been reached. It moves forward when the counselor disagrees with the belief or beliefs of the client, and when the client decides to question these beliefs himself at the urging of the counselor. A counselor, for example, who believes that he can be angered by another person will hardly be able to help a client who also holds that belief. Instruction, counseling, or psychotherapy is at an end when total agreement between the two parties exists.

For ministers, self-blame and perfectionism, although very common traits for the community at large, are reinforced products of their theological training as well. Claims that this is as it should be, may be strenuously refuted.

Despite the Christian message of man's fallibility and God's forgiveness, it is the exceptional minister who would not severely blame himself for murder, theft, or an immoral sexual act. Yet, if he believes that man is weak and that God has infinite powers of forgiveness, why should he hate himself for being imperfect and not forgive himself when God is willing to do so? There is regrettably more lip service than substance to these beliefs. Why else would a clergyman ever feel guilt and depression? When found in him they are no less signs of neurosis than when occurring in others.

2. Candid communication with a clergyman is frequently difficult. Through no particular wish of his own, the minister has been envisioned as a pure, holy, unsullied messenger from heaven whose ears cannot, have not, and should not be dirtied with indelicate speech. Because of this perception held by the layman, the minister is, for example, often spared discussion of problems that arouse shame. He is also usually spared the use of profanity by his clients. In their normal moods clients may often swear in order to express themselves fully, and this is often done using God's name in vain. But in the presence of a minister rough language is contained, lest it offend him.

This is regrettable, of course, as it tends to prevent certain persons from counseling with the clergy. The supermasculine construction laborer and the juvenile delinquent want to speak freely in their vernacular, much of it consisting of profanity. Many ministers do counsel such persons, of course, but I believe that swearing or taboo subjects will not offend them or make them dislike the speaker.

This is not to be taken as a plea for profanity but rather as a plea for accepting the client as he is. It is also a plea to the clergy to undo this imposed image if they are to reach the widest range of persons.

3. Sinners often feel inferior and unworthy in the presence of a holy man. They already imagine their transgressions to be so much more serious than the sins of others. This is especially the case when they are in the presence of what they conceive to be a near sinless person, the minister. This is an advantage in many cases, since it spurs some persons on to a more ethical life. But if the gap between the minister's perfection as imagined by the sinner and the sinner's imagined despicableness is too great, there is not likely to be the sort of relationship that will elicit the kind of uncovering needed in counseling. Just as a beginning golfer does not enjoy a game with a pro, so too a grievous sinner can feel more, not less, discomfort by being in the presence of light and purity. One need only imagine the agonizing discomfort an alcoholic rapist would experience were he to counsel with the pope. Every minister carries some of this aura for some people. Again, this is due to no fault of his own, though the fact remains that here too he cannot be his most efficient self.

4. The clergy are notoriously weak in their knowledge of science and the scientific method. This brings up the old struggle of faith versus reason. The clergyman has been losing this struggle, not because one of these deserves a higher priority than the other, but because he refuses to recognize the point at which one displaces the other. Most thinking persons do not dispute such long-standing scientific facts as the age of the earth, or evolution, etc. Yet some ministers still insist on the six-day creation story. Such literal adherence to past beliefs may well serve to undermine the respect that he receives from the educated and enlightened client. Modern man is slowly learning

to be rational, objective, demanding of proof, and considerate of alternate hypotheses. As this trend continues he will be asking himself questions which never occurred to his father. Unless the pastor too is willing to keep abreast of the times, he may lose this intelligent audience. Unless he can offer sound reasoning or proof for his statements, rather than dogmatic creeds, he will continue to experience more and more alienation from the thinking people.

When Pastors Succeed as Counselors

The foregoing remarks need cause no dismay to those aspiring to do counseling. Some of the disadvantages the pastor lives under can be corrected. The remainder will have to be lived with. Happily, the minister also has a number of advantages that his position as a clergyman gives him in the pursuit of counseling.

1. The pastor's motives in counseling are more nearly altruistic than are the motives of any other profession. He carries on his work for the love of God and the good of the client's soul. If he can be handsomely rewarded for his efforts, so much the better. But financial considerations as a rule play little or no role in the reasons why a pastor counsels. His time is devoted freely and willingly. I have known ministers who have kept doctors' hours and spent freely of their meager funds to be of help.

One who gives this degree of service in an unselfish and uncomplaining manner cannot but impress a client. Such devotion is rare among us professionals. Our time must be paid for. An appointment not kept is usually charged for. Counseling over the telephone is discouraged. Money is never loaned. And our cars are not available for taxi service. There is much merit in this hard-boiled approach. Nevertheless, one has to admire unselfish devotion —even though it may at times backfire.

Clients have rightly accused some psychotherapists of encouraging them to continue in treatment past the point where it was necessary. Such accusations make little sense when applied to the minister. He is only too glad to be able to terminate counseling, since he receives no fees if he counsels members of his church. This is how the majority of pastoral counseling is being done today. A movement is afoot whereby a minister with extensive training in counseling is hired by a church or group of churches and is paid a fee for his services. This practice may continue to grow, but for many years yet we may confidently expect the local minister to counsel his own, and not for a price.

These magnanimous actions by pastors serve them in good stead in counseling for another reason. The average client has a good deal of inferiority feeling to contend with, for his sense of unworthiness runs deep indeed. This can be countered somewhat by showing him through actions that you, the minister, think he is worth all the effort. You write a letter in his behalf; you make a trip for him; you help him secure a job. Such actions cannot, except in rare instances, fail to make some impact on this feeling, which the client has, that he is all bad. He cannot but wonder why such unselfish efforts are being made in his behalf, unless it is because his pastor sees more in him than he sees in himself.

2. The pastor can be more confident in his beliefs than other professionals. Most believe that the Bible was divinely inspired and contains the final truth in all matters of morals and faith. It would be extremely difficult not to be completely at ease with such material if one believed it was literally the word of God. In such a situation, the

minister should never feel the slightest qualm over his doctrine nor the minutest doubt that he is correct. What an enviable position!

3. By training and experience the pastor has much skill in instruction. I hope it will be clear by this point that rational counseling is essentially a teaching experience. To reiterate: the counseling hour is likened to a lesson, the counselor to a teacher, the client to a student, the office to a classroom. In short, the whole experience we have been describing is a didactic one.

And who, other than the professional teacher, is better qualified to teach? Who has as many lectures to prepare? Who addresses more people each week? Certainly it is not the hospital psychiatrist, who ministers from behind his desk or makes his rounds of the wards. Certainly it is not the clinical psychologist, who tests, plans research, and teaches only an occasional university course or gives a talk to the PTA. Generally speaking, the pastor is cast more often in the role of instructor to more people than are his colleagues.

Doing *this* kind of counseling places him in his natural milieu. If he can learn to use reason in counseling, he can have every confidence that he will do it well, for it calls for the same familiar skills that he already has.

4. If he adheres to the psychologically sound precepts of the gospel, the pastor will find himself on familiar ground. Rational counseling should, therefore, come very easily to him, for it is basically in harmony with many of Christianity's most prized beliefs. The fact that there is not perfect agreement should not deter him from recognizing the similarity between rational thinking and Scripture. Again the pastor has a head start, so to speak, over other counselors, in that the commitment of the latter

to these philosophies is seldom as intense as his.

The minister has long been taught, and he has long been practicing, the advice of Paul that recommends that we be content with our lot (Phil. 4:11). This is essentially the same as the principle in psychology that states that we cannot be made disturbed by our frustrations—that we *can* bear our burdens with equanimity. Religion has taught this all along, while for years psychology has taught the frustration-aggression hypothesis, which postulated anger as the *inevitable* consequence of frustration.[35] A minister who has been practicing his faith is living proof against the findings of these respected investigators.

We could cite numerous other examples demonstrating that rational-emotive psychotherapy has supported Scripture and is compatible with much theological belief. Our emphasis on not blaming people for their errors is a particularly strong case in point. The devout minister who has taken Christ's counsel literally does not blame others or himself, and he does not punish out of revenge. This is psychologically sound and Christian as well.

The whole Christian message of not judging others, loving those who hurt us, not reproving a scorner, forgiving those who trespass against us, loving our enemies, and not being overcome with evil are all principles of modern rational-emotive psychotherapy. The psychological counselor advises the client to love his neurotic mate and to forgive her for her rantings, to love the sinner but not the sin, to guard himself against committing the emotional faults he finds in others, to accept himself as an imperfect product who can still enjoy life despite these imperfections.

Here are principles in high agreement with Christianity. The pastoral counselor who wonders whether he is qualified to counsel need only realize this close relationship between religion and psychology. If he is a conscientious minister, he can also be an able psychotherapist. Here is truly a marriage, not totally harmonious to be sure, but nevertheless a marriage that can grow and become fruitful over the years if each mate will recognize the merits in the teachings of the other.

A word will need to be said to the clergyman who judges this therapeutic system by its founder. It is ironic that Albert Ellis, who holds such unorthodox views on religion and sex, should be the one to offer us a system that touches at numerous points the heart of Christian conduct. The fact that it does so can easily be overlooked by the short-sighted. Errors of overgeneralization will be made abundantly. The halo effect is sure to work in a negative direction in this area. *All* of Ellis' thinking is likely to be condemned by the alarmist because *some* of it will doubtless be very distasteful to the clergy at large. This would be a regrettable mistake, for the ministry would be the loser. Every man has something worthwhile to contribute, even though that single gem of a contribution is surrounded by meaner stuff. So it is with Ellis. So it was with Freud. He too was an atheist and unhappily insisted on labeling much behavior as sexual. For years many persons failed to recognize many of his greatest discoveries because they judged all of his work on the basis of what, to them, were other highly objectionable views. Today, ministers have finally accepted many of Freud's theories. The fact that he was an atheist is ignored, and his work is now judged on its own merits.

An indication of the maturity of the clergy will be the achievement of the same objectivity toward rational-emotive therapy that they have adopted toward psychoanalysis.

Bibliography and Notes

Bibliography

Abbott, Walter M. (ed.), *The Documents of Vatican II.* The Guild Press, 1966.

Alexander, Franz, and Ross, Helen, *Dynamic Psychiatry.* The University of Chicago Press, 1952.

Barker, R., *et al.,* "Frustration and Regression: An Experiment with Young Children," *University of Iowa Studies in Child Welfare,* Vol. XVIII, No. 1 (1941).

Bartemeier, L. H., *Urban America and the Planning of Mental Health Services.* Group for the Advancement of Psychiatry, 1964.

Bateson, G., "The Frustration-Aggression Hypothesis and Culture," *Psychological Review,* Vol. XLVIII (1941), pp. 350-355.

Brown, J. F., and Menninger, Karl A., *The Psychodynamics of Abnormal Behavior.* McGraw-Hill Book Company, Inc., 1940.

Cannon, Walter B., *The Wisdom of the Body.* W. W. Norton & Company, Inc., 1932.

Carnegie, Dale, *How to Win Friends and Influence People.* Simon and Schuster, 1936.

Dunlap, Knight, *Personal Adjustment.* McGraw-Hill Book Company, Inc., 1946.

Durant, Will, *The Story of Civilization,* Vol. III, *Caesar and Christ.* Simon and Schuster, 1944.

Ellis, Albert, *How to Live with a Neurotic.* Crown Publishers, 1957.

Ellis, Albert, and Harper, Robert A., *A Guide to Rational Living.* Prentice-Hall, Inc., 1961.

Ellis, Albert, *Reason and Emotion in Psychotherapy.* Lyle Stuart, 1962.

Freud, Sigmund, *The Problem of Anxiety.* W. W. Norton & Company, Inc., 1936.

Goldstein, Kurt, *The Organism.* American Book Company, 1939.

Gutheil, Emilian A., "Reactive Depressions," in Silvano Arieti (ed.), *American Handbook of Psychiatry,* Vol. I. Basic Books, 1959.

Hauck, Paul A., *The Rational Management of Children.* Libra Press, 1967.

Hauck, Paul A., "The Neurotic Agreement in Psychotherapy," *Rational Living,* Vol. I (1966), pp. 31-34.

Herman, Emily, *Creative Prayer.* Harper and Brothers, 1924.

Kierkegaard, Sören, *The Concept of Dread.* Princeton University Press, 1944.

May, Rollo, *The Meaning of Anxiety.* Ronald Press, 1957.

Menninger, Karl A., *The Human Mind.* Alfred A. Knopf, Inc., 1948.

Miller, N. E., *et al.,* "Frustration and Aggression," *Psychological Review,* Vol. XLVIII (1941), pp. 337-340.

Peale, Norman Vincent, *The Power of Positive Thinking.* Prentice-Hall, 1952.

Peale, Norman Vincent, "Love Thyself First," *This Week Magazine, Minneapolis Tribune,* Sept. 5, 1965.

Portnoy, I., "The Anxiety States," in Silvano Arieti (ed.), *American Handbook of Psychiatry,* Vol. I. Basic Books, 1957.

Ridenour, Nina B., *Mental Health in the United States: A Fifty-Year History.* Harvard University Press, 1961.

Sahakian, William S. (ed.), *Psychopathology Today.* F. E. Peacock Publishers, Inc., 1970.

Sears, R., *et al.,* "Minor Studies in Aggression: I. Measurement of Aggressive Behavior," *Journal of Psychology,* Vol. IX (1940), pp. 227-281.

Sheiner, S., *The Fear of Anxiety.* The Auxiliary Council to the Association for the Advancement of Psychoanalysis, 1953.

Simpson, George G., *The Meaning of Evolution.* Yale University Press, 1949.

Sullivan, Harry Stack, *The Interpersonal Theory of Psychiatry,* ed. by Helen S. Perry and Mary Gawel. W. W. Norton & Company, Inc., 1953.

Szasz, Thomas S., "Mental Illness Is Not Disease," in *Abnormal Psychology,* ed. by E. A. Southwell and H. Feldman. Wadsworth Publishing Co., 1969.

Weatherhead, Leslie D., *The Christian Agnostic.* Abingdon Press, 1965.

Notes

1. Ridenour, *Mental Health in the United States.* Cf. also Bartemeier, *Urban America and the Planning of Mental Health Services.*

2. Ellis, *How to Live with a Neurotic,* p. 9.

3. Dunlap, *Personal Adjustment.* Cf. also Brown and Menninger, *The Psychodynamics of Abnormal Behavior,* and Menninger, *The Human Mind,* pp. 335-341.

4. Ellis, *Reason and Emotion in Psychotherapy,* pp. 60-88. Cf. also Szasz, "Mental Illness Is Not Disease," in *Abnormal Psychology,* by Southwell and Feldman, Ch. 1, pp. 5-11.

5. Ellis, *Reason and Emotion in Psychotherapy,* pp. 60-88.

6. "Pastoral Constitution on the Church in the Modern World," in Abbott (ed.), *The Documents of Vatican II,* p. 269.

7. Durant, *The Story of Civilization,* Vol. III, *Caesar and Christ,* p. 34.

8. Ellis, *How to Live with a Neurotic.*

9. Ellis and Harper, *A Guide to Rational Living.*

10. Hauck, *The Rational Management of Children.*

11. Carnegie, *How to Win Friends and Influence People.*

12. Peale, *The Power of Positive Thinking.*

13. Peale, "Love Thyself First," *This Week Magazine, Minneapolis Tribune,* Sept. 5, 1965.

14. Sahakian, *Psychopathology Today,* p. 390.

15. Gutheil, "Reactive Depressions," in S. Arieti (ed.), *American Handbook of Psychiatry,* Vol. I, pp. 345-352.

16. Sahakian, *op. cit.,* p. 389.

17. O. H. Mowrer, *The Crisis in Psychiatry and Religion* (D. Van Nostrand Company, Inc., 1961), pp. 81-102.
18. Goldstein, *The Organism.*
19. Cannon, *The Wisdom of the Body.*
20. Simpson, *The Meaning of Evolution.*
21. Kierkegaard, *The Concept of Dread.*
22. Freud, *The Problem of Anxiety.*
23. Sullivan, *The Interpersonal Theory of Psychiatry,* ed. by Perry and Gawel, pp. 113-115.
24. May, *The Meaning of Anxiety.*
25. Menninger, *op. cit.*
26. Portnoy, "The Anxiety States," in Arieti (ed.), *American Handbook of Psychiatry,* Vol. I.
27. May, *op. cit.*
28. Sheiner, *The Fear of Anxiety.*
29. Alexander and Ross, *Dynamic Psychiatry.*
30. Brown and Menninger, *op. cit.,* pp. 131-132.
31. Herman, *Creative Prayer.* Cf. also Weatherhead, *The Christian Agnostic.*
32. Herman, *op. cit.*
33. Miller *et al.,* "Frustration and Aggression," *Psychological Review,* Vol. XLVIII (1941), pp. 337-340.
34. Hauck, "The Neurotic Agreement in Psychotherapy," *Rational Living,* Vol. I (1966), pp. 31-34.
35. Miller, *loc. cit.* Cf. also the following: Sears *et al.,* "Minor Studies in Aggression: I. Measurement of Aggressive Behavior," *Journal of Psychology,* Vol. IX (1940), pp. 227-281; Bateson, "The Frustration-Aggression Hypothesis and Culture," *Psychological Review,* Vol. XLVIII (1941), pp. 350-355; Barker *et al.,* "Frustration and Regression: An Experiment with Young Children," *University of Iowa Studies in Child Welfare,* Vol. XVIII, No. 1 (1941).